D0168810

Karma & Karma Yoga

With kind regards, ॐ and prem

Karma & Karma Yoga

Swami Niranjanananda Saraswati

*Discourses from the Yogadrishti (Yogavision) series
of satsangs at Ganga Darshan Vishwa Yogapeeth,
Munger, from 25th to 28th February 2010*

Yoga Publications Trust, Munger, Bihar, India

© Bihar School of Yoga 2010

All rights reserved. No part of this publication may be reproduced, transmitted or stored in a retrieval system, in any form or by any means, without permission in writing from Yoga Publications Trust.

The terms Satyananda Yoga® and Bihar Yoga® are registered trademarks owned by International Yoga Fellowship Movement (IYFM). The use of the same in this book is with permission and should not in any way be taken as affecting the validity of the marks.

Published by Yoga Publications Trust
    First edition 2010

ISBN: 978-81-86336-85-4

Publisher and distributor: Yoga Publications Trust, Ganga Darshan, Munger, Bihar, India.

Website: www.biharyoga.net
         www.rikhiapeeth.net

Printed at Aegean Offset Printers, Greater Noida

Dedication

*To our guru Sri Swami Satyananda Saraswati
who continues to inspire and guide us
on our spiritual journey.*

Contents

Karma and Karma Yoga

25th February 2010

The theme for this satsang series is karma and karma yoga. In order to understand karma and karma yoga, we have to first understand their basic concept. We have to consider them not just as action and reaction, but as expressions and experiences of life, as conditions of life.

Origin of karma

The word karma comes from the Sanskrit root *krit*, which means performance of an action. Both 'kriya' and 'karma' are derived from the root krit. *Kriya* means activity and *karma* not only means action but also manifestation. Generally people translate the word karma as action, but in actuality karma is manifestation of human nature. It is something which is expressed spontaneously, naturally and unconditionally, and this entire creation is nothing but manifestation of karma. The entire creation, the entire universe, the entire life is manifestation of karma, and the seed of karma in creation was planted by the cosmic will.

Imagine the unmanifest dimension, and from there move outwards towards the manifest dimension. Where does karma originate? When there was nothing in the world, just infinite eternal space, creation did not exist, then there was only a thought. And that thought was wrapped up in space. And space is considered Supreme.

The Vedas say, "Kham Brahman". *Kham* refers to the space element, and this space has been called *Brahman*, Supreme, as it is the basis of all other elements and evolutes, and is ever-expanding. In that eternal space a pulsation of energy takes place in the form of a thought, an idea: "I am one. I want to become many." The emergence of this vibration in space indicates the beginning of the karmic process. The seed of karma is planted with a thought, a vibration. And the thought contains the desire for multiplicity. How will 'one' become 'many'? Through what method, what act, what expression? The moment you think 'many', you are implying multiplication. And multiplication is an action; it is creation, performance, expression. Therefore, the basic seed of creation is karma: "I want to see myself in many forms. I want to multiply myself. I want to manifest myself." Once the seed is planted, then to give it a manifest form, energy is released.

Energy and consciousness are the two eternal principles of life. These two become the basis of the world and the work of creation begins. Through karma life evolves, creation expands and the universe is formed. And at the time of dissolution, it is through karma that all these are destroyed.

The manifest creation, the manifest nature is known as Prakriti in Sanskrit. *Pra* is the prefix indicating the highest, the best, the strongest; *krit* indicates performance or expression, and '*i*' at the end represents the energy or shakti factor. So the literal meaning of the word *prakriti* is the energy, the power through which the highest and the best expression or performance can manifest.

Prakriti is the force responsible for the emergence of the universe and of life in all its varieties. When life emerges from Prakriti, it is subject to the law of karma. Everything in this creation is subject to the law of karma. There is nothing which is free from karma. The tree which grows is bound by karma, the sun that shines is bound by karma, the fire that burns is bound by karma. The wind that blows is subject to karma. Animals are subjects to karma, insects fly and crawl

because of karma. Human beings live because of karma. The universes, galaxies and planets are created, survive and destroyed because of karma.

It has been said in the scriptures, *Samsariti iti samsarah* – "That which crawls, that which moves is samsara". The indication of movement here is connected with kriya, and kriya and karma are the laws of creation. Every being in creation undergoes the process of karma; the bacteria, an animal, a bird, a tree, a rock and a human being. The difference is that a human being knows that he is performing karma due to his faculty of intelligence while the other creatures do not know. But, this understanding is faulty. We are aware that something is being done by us and call that doing karma. We associate karma with the senses and believe that karma is performed through the agency of the senses. However, karma is not performed by the senses; the principle of karma makes the senses perform the appropriate karma required in life. The senses do not possess independent intelligence; the principle, law and discipline of karma makes the senses, body and mind perform karma, and that is what we perceive. Thus the visible, perceptible world which a human being can experience through the senses is suffused with karma.

Karma, however, has a companion without which it cannot act itself out, cannot manifest itself. While this companion exists, Prakriti performs karma, we perform karma, the universe performs karma, but if this companion is not there, karmas cannot be executed properly. This companion is called dharma. The whole creation performs karma according to its dharma. *Dharma* means appropriateness or order. It is not religion or a religious concept, and was only associated with religion much later, but when karma was born, dharma also took birth. They are twins and they assist each other. Look at nature, everything in nature takes place according to an order, a dharma. A tree grows according to its dharma, seasons change according to dharma. Karma and dharma, performance and order, are the two foundations of life and creation.

How do we understand karma in the manifest world? It is not actually necessary to understand it in the unmanifest dimension, as karma is only an expression of knowledge there – we don't need to know the how and why of that. What we need to understand, what we need to look at, is our own life. The karmas that are appearing and guiding each and every person in their life need to be understood and handled. When we are able to handle our own life, then it is not difficult to understand the principles of karma in the unmanifest dimension. So, how do the karmas manifest in our life?

4

The software of karma

When we acquire this body, it comes with an operating software. Initially, when you buy a computer it comes loaded with the basic operating system software – Windows or Apple. It is that basic software which allows you to feed in other softwares to make them and the computer itself useful. In the same way, this life is an expression of karma, and karma comes with a software to facilitate its expression in life.

For example, a hotelier will use the software which is appropriate for hotel management. The hotel software gives the number of rooms, the number of beds, how many people have come and gone, whether they have paid or not, what they have had at the restaurant, and so on. The hotel software is specific to hotels. Business software is specific to business, educational software is specific to education, diagnostic software is specific to diagnosis. In the same manner, the basic operating system software with which we have come into this life is karma.

The operating system software of karma contains four different backend softwares. The first backend software is the basic instincts – *ahara* or craving, *nidra* or sleep, *bhaya* or insecurities and fears, and *maithuna* or gross sensuality and sexuality.

The second backend software of karma is *swabhava*, the nature, the character that our mind expresses in life. The third backend software is *samskaras*, impressions that we carry forward from the past. And the fourth backend software is performance of the senses. These are the backend softwares and we come equipped with them into this life. They are given by Prakriti, by the shakti, the force responsible for creation, manifestation and expression of the cosmic will.

Consciousness and energy

There are two elements governing life: consciousness and energy. In tantra they are known as Shiva and Shakti, in Vedanta as Brahman and Maya, in Samkhya as Purusha and Prakriti.

Consciousness can see, observe, feel, think and plan, but cannot implement. Whereas energy cannot see, think or plan, but it can implement. They have been described as two people, one blind and the other lame. Consciousness is lame, but it can see; it has eyes, but no legs. Energy is blind, it cannot see, but has legs. These are the two elements which are responsible for creation and for our life.

Consciousness can plan, see and analyze, but cannot implement without the assistance, help and support of Shakti. A question: if a blind person and a lame person wanted to come to this program, how would they come? The lame will sit on the shoulders of the blind and direct the blind to walk. The blind will depend on the vision of the lame for guidance and direction. In order to fulfil a role and a purpose, they both have to help each other. In the same way, consciousness and energy help, support and assist each other.

Consciousness, or Shiva, sits on the shoulders of Shakti and points the way. And energy, Shakti, has to follow the directions of consciousness, Shiva. Karma is the name of consciousness and energy interacting together and directing life. When karma integrates with an individual, a life form, the consciousness and energy create a backend system software in the personality of the life form.

Everything has its software, including trees and animals. Swami Sivananda used to say consciousness sleeps in stones, dreams in plants, begins to awaken in animals and can be fully realized in man. Consciousness and energy exist in each and every object of creation. Nothing can be created without them. Even a rock, a piece of stone, has consciousness in it. Quantum physics describes how the consciousness in a stone can be awakened by connecting with the energy centre of the stone. Consciousness and energy in the form of Shiva and Shakti create life, and they put softwares in life which are guided by karma.

The first set of software consists of the basic instincts, the second set is the mental nature, the third set is the impressions of the mind, the samskaras in the psyche, and the fourth set is the function of the senses. All these backend softwares are known by different names, but they are associated with karma. Although one cannot exist without karmas as they are the guiding principles of life, their direction can be changed, and that is the effort that a spiritual aspirant makes.

Karma in the life of Swami Satyananda

When Swami Satyananda, our guru, was being initiated in sannyasa by his guru, Swami Sivananda, he asked a question. "What are my obligations after taking sannyasa? Do I avoid my karmas?"

There is a belief that one has to wilfully transcend the karmas, one has to wilfully be free from them. However, remember that the moment you free yourself from karma, you won't remain in this creation any more. The nature of this creation is karmic, so how can you live in this creation without karma? That is what Swami Sivananda told him.

One cannot exhaust karma in the normal conditions or environment. Swami Sivananda said, "After sannyasa you

shall carry on with the normal karmas which you have been performing till today – working in the office, the kitchen, the publications department, tying packets, sweeping the floor, the secretarial work. Nothing is going to change." Then Swami Satyananda said, "Well, if nothing is going to change, then instead of performing karma here I may as well go back home and work there. It will help some people in my home." Swami Sivananda told him, "Yes, you can do that but when you perform karma at home, you are doing it for your own pleasure, fulfilment and satisfaction; you are performing it with certain expectations and you will be affected by the outcome of that karma. Success will elate you and failure will frustrate you. When you perform karma in the ashram, you will not be doing it for your own gratification nor will you have any expectation from it. What you do in the ashram you offer to the guru. The success of the karma will be guru's and its failure will also be guru's. You are free and you will begin to think, 'I have been told to do this, therefore I am doing it. It is not the success or failure that I am interested in. It is the positive and creative expression that is required of me.'"

It is the positive and creative action and expression that you focus on in the ashram while being engaged in karma. The karmas do not change; only the inner understanding, the mental perception changes. With this understanding and perceptional change, eventually one can become aware of all the different ties and knots of karma, and release them one by one. Swami Satyananda asked Swami Sivananda, "How will I know that I have fulfilled my karmic duties?" Swami Sivananda told him, "When karmas are over, you will know. When the night comes you know that the sun is not there any more. Similarly, when you are free from karma you will know that you are free. If I tie you up, you will know that you are bound and if I untie you, you will know that you are free. It is an experience." So Swami Satyananda embarked upon the path of karma yoga with full determination and devotion.

There are many sannyasins, here and in the world, who shun karma and try to meditate. There are sannyasins here who have been trying to practise many hours of meditation every day in order to attain self-realization and who still get disturbed by a karma and the responses and reactions of a karma. I am saying this to all sannyasins: you have had the example of your own guru and yet you have been blind to how he has lived his life and what he has taught. If you have been blind up to now, there is no hope or scope for you to attain vision. If you have the ability to see the inspirational life that our guru has lived, then all the answers are there. For me all my answers lie in the life of my guru, not in the scriptures. I get all my answers when I observe the life of my own guru.

He embarked upon a constant journey through karmas. When he was here he did not have the time to practise his meditations, his yoga. He did not practise meditation or yoga for twenty years in the manner that you are used to or you practise. His whole life was living yoga. From 1963 to 1983 Swami Satyananda focused on the karmas for establishing the yoga movement with the understanding and awareness that it was not for personal gratification, but for clearing his own external karmas in life. Thus, when he established Ganga Darshan Vishwa Yogapeeth, this monument of yoga, he knew that one chapter had concluded; he had crossed one hurdle of the karmas. Then he left it and never looked back, eventually settling in Rikhia. It was in Rikhia that he did his sadhana, his meditations, his tapasyas, his austerities. He did not do it in Munger, in Ganga Darshan. He did them only when he knew that he had overcome the greatest obstacles that karma can put before an individual – obstacles of egos, desires, ambitions, of name and fame.

From my observation, I can tell you that all the karmic bondages from the life of Swami Satyananda were removed in the year 2003. For six years, between 2003 and 2009, he lived as a person not bound by karma, but as a *jivanmukta*, one who is freed from life and its bondages. As a jivanmukta, his name shines now in the roll of the other jivanmuktas such as Markandeya, Shukadev and Dattatreya. These are the people who had cut every bondage of karma from their life and were one with the cosmos. Swami Satyananda could have left his body after exhausting his karmas in 2003. Once you are free from the bondages of karma in life, you can live eternally or call death instantly – one has that power. Swami Satyananda lived for these six years in order to strengthen the sannyasa tradition, the identity of a disciple and a sadhana for future generations of visionaries.

Karma can be exhausted only through karma, not through sadhana, dhyana, mantra and austerities. Those who are unable to exhaust their karmas have to get involved in the world even after their sadhana and austerities.

Karma is the software of life without which you would not be here, I would not be here, you would not be thinking what you are thinking now, I would not be speaking what I am speaking now, you would not have any aspirations, ambitions or desires to achieve anything in life, and I would not have any aspirations or inclination to interact with anyone. So, the karma software is in four parts – the instincts, the nature, the impressions and the senses. When one has gone through all these four levels of karma, then one is freed from the gross karmic bondage. Sri Swamiji's life exemplifies this.

Basic instincts

The first level of karma includes the four basic instincts: craving, sleep, fear and sexuality. Craving is for our satisfaction. Our body craves nourishment, our mind craves nourishment, our spirit craves nourishment, our emotions crave nourishment, and this craving is known as ahara or feeding. Feeding the body, the senses, the mind, the emotions. This feeding begins from the day of our birth and goes on to the last day of our life. This instinct is for experiencing a feeling of happiness, enjoyment, contentment and fulfilment. Our search in life is limited to that. This feeding fuels the fire just as when we put ghee on fire, the flames rise higher. When you feed your senses, your body, your mind, the flames of desire highten. The only way not to have the ahara fire is to throw a bucket of water on it, which very few people want to do.

The second instinct is sleep, nidra. The instinct nidra is also active from day one till the last day of our life. People spend fifty percent of their lives sleeping. It is the instinct with the biggest influence in life. It is a karma.

Similarly, insecurity, fear or bhaya is a karma, a software. When you see that your zone of comfort is being disturbed, fears come in. When you see that you are going to lose something, insecurities come in. Whenever you see that there is going to be loss, insecurities and fears present themselves in your life. That is a karma.

Sexuality is another part of karma. It represents the need to propagate.

The instincts are the four basic backend programming with which we come into this life. They control and guide all our responses and behaviours throughout our journey. When they dominate and control life we are attracted towards materialistic gains, external gains. They carry us through our life until we are able to replace the old software with newer ones.

11

IN SUMMARY

1. Cosmic karma

The entire creation, the universe, the galaxies, are the result of a cosmic karma. It is a karma arising out of interaction between consciousness and energy, which is eternal and all-pervasive. In consciousness there is generation of idea, thought and expectation. We are an outcome of that cosmic interaction which took place in remote antiquity before creation. Creation was the product of consciousness and energy interacting with each other. Life is a product of consciousness and energy interacting with each other. Behaviour and human response is a product of consciousness and energy.

Creation is the outcome of a karma which is cosmic in nature and, as limited beings, we cannot understand the logic or reasoning behind the cosmic karma. The fact is that we are here because of that cosmic karma. In the final conclusion we are not the masters of our life. That is the conclusion given by the scriptures and saints. Thus, karma means expression, it does not just mean action. Everything that is being experienced and expressed in life is karma.

2. Software of life

We are not the doer, we are only actors. And we act according to the software which governs life. The example of a computer illustrates this. A computer comes with one simple operating system; its hard drive is empty, only the operating system is there. That operating system can be Win 7, Windows XP, Windows 97 or Windows 95. The operating systems also keep evolving.

Once you receive the computer you can install the required software to meet your needs. If you are a movie director, you need to have the appropriate software with which you can create movies. If you are a scientist, you need to have the right software to assist in your calculations. If you are a hotelier, you need the specific software to manage your hotel. Different additional softwares are installed according to different needs, but originally it came with a basic operating system. In the same manner, in this life we have also come with a basic operating system.

3. The operating system

The first component of the basic system software are the four instincts. They are responsible for creation of karmas in this life. Craving is an instinct which creates karma, sleep creates karma, sensuality and passion are responsible for creation of karma, fears and insecurities are responsible for creation of karma.

The second software is the inherent nature, which does not change. The nature of a lemon tree is to produce lemons, not mangoes or bananas. The nature of a mango tree is to produce mangoes, not apricots or oranges. The inherent nature in a personality will always manifest. If you are aware of your nature, if you transcend it, you will know one aspect of karma. Whether you are arrogant, humble, complicated, simple, enlightened, materialistic, sensitive, strong, you know what your nature is. This is a major karma you have been living.

The third software is samskaras, the impressions within the consciousness which we receive as a package and which become the building block of our life. That is the third operating system.

The fourth operating system includes the senses and the application and association of the senses with other sense objects in search of happiness, pleasure, contentment and fulfilment. Senses also become a part of the human karma.

We are born with these operating systems in our computer. Different softwares are fed in as and when required, choices which are created by our culture, tradition, society, family, gurus and teachers. At different times in our life we use these different softwares to elevate, uplift and clear the path.

We receive a basic operating system at the time of birth which we live here in this life. After all, we have received this beautiful instrument, this computer, which comes with its basic operating system but, depending on our inclination, we can use one particular software to move forward in life. I came down into the world with a basic operating system, but then my guru fed in me a new software of sannyasa and I am living that. I am expressing that. The basic software allows me to live and experience the life and the new additional software allows me to express myself as I would like to see myself, and inspires me to reach that point where I can be myself.

4. Freedom from karma

Is it possible to become totally free from the karmas in this life? Yes, but not for you. For me, yes. Because your path and destiny are different from my path and destiny. You are here for a few days, then you will go back to your friends, family, society, profession, home, likes, dislikes, ambitions. Coming here is only a pastime for you; your actual life is lived outside. Therefore, you can't be a saint. You can be a *grihastha*, a social person. As a grihastha you can go only so far because that path will take you only that far, which is to make you a better social person, a *sadgrihastha*. Beyond that, don't have any expectation from yourself as long as you are outside in the world with your duties, responsibilities, attachments and environment.

It is incorrect and inappropriate to presume that a grihastha can become like a sannyasin. Your path is different, my path is different. You have your commitments and obligations which are social. I don't have those commitments, neither to family, nor to material possessions. This ashram is not mine. I can leave it in the blink of an eye if I have to. But a householder cannot leave their home, no matter how hard they try.

Freedom from karma is only attained by those who have renounced or developed detachment from everything around them. Nothing influences them. When this kind of detachment takes place from karma, then two states are attained. One is of *videhamukti*, freedom from the confines of the senses, and the other is of jivanmukti, freedom from the bondage of karma in life.

As a social person you can only go up to freedom from the sensory attractions, not beyond it. No matter how much you meditate, or how much time you spend in the ashram, the condition in which you are living and growing in will only allow you to become free from the influences of the senses. Whereas a sannyasin is alone, nobody in front, nobody behind, nobody on top, nobody below. If we are determined and convinced, and make the necessary effort, then we can attain jivanmukti, freedom from life, as there is nothing to tie us to the ground except guru and God.

Swami Satyananda proved that. He was free from his karmas in the year 2003 and for six years he lived as a jivanmukta, a person whom life or the attractions of life cannot bind or hold any more. This indicates a state of mind where you have overcome the state of *abhinivesha*, the fear of losing one's identity and dying. Nobody wants to die. Everyone fears death forgetting that birth is one spectrum of life and death is another spectrum of life. All are chasing a mirage of water in the desert and this is the failure of understanding in people who do not understand the principles of spiritual life. However, freedom from karma is attainable by a sannyasin as a jivanmukta and by a social person as a videhamukta.

Gunas and Karma

26th February 2010

We come into this life with the basic operating system which provides the experience of life with all its expressions. The components of the operating system are: the four instincts – ahara, nidra, bhaya and maithuna; *swabhava* or the character, the nature with which we come into this life; *samskaras*, the impressions which we carry forward from our previous lives; and the senses, and the association of the senses with sense objects.

Influence of gunas

The four components are also affected, guided and nurtured by the three *gunas* or qualities: sattwa, rajas and tamas. Our samskaras, sensory interactions, swabhava and instincts can be sattwic, rajasic and tamasic, or a mix of the three.

The three gunas are cosmic in nature which manifest as the support system for the basic operating system of our life. At the cosmic level, they are the qualities which are latent and inherent in creation. What is the inherent and latent quality in a seed? If you open the seed up you don't see the tree, the leaves, flowers or fruits, but if you plant the seed and provide the right care, the seed will sprout. Open the seed, you see nothing. In that nothingness is the latent possibility for the growth of a plant. When the time and conditions are right, the seed dies and the plant appears. The seed has to die for the sprout to emerge. In the same

17

manner, the seed of ego and individuality within us has to die for spiritual awakening to take place. Just as within the seed is contained the possibility for the growth of the plant, the inherent possibility and the potential of the qualities which are the support systems exist at the cosmic dimension. They are called the gunas. However, at the cosmic level they are in absolute harmony and peace in their basic nature.

Nature of gunas

What is the basic nature or quality of the three gunas – sattwa, rajas and tamas? The quality of sattwa is luminosity, illumination, wisdom, understanding, knowledge, creativity, simplicity, innocence of the head and simplicity of the heart. The quality or nature of rajas is creation, manifestation, transformation, change, activity, expression and performance. The nature of tamas is a conditioned, defined state of body and mind. The conditionings in life indicate the nature of tamas.

When creation is born, when Prakriti begins to do its work, then what emerges is a form. The identity of the entire universe as well as individual life is perceived through form. How would I know that you exist? Only when your form is seen. Where there is no form, one may imagine the existence of an object, but imagination is not proof. The proof of existence is form. The state where form and shape are established is the state of tamo guna. It is like creating a pot out of undifferentiated clay. Tamo guna does not indicate negativity, but the assumption of a state or condition. This body with its form and shape is tamasic. The trees, the sun, the stars and planets also indicate tamas. When the unmanifest becomes manifest and assumes a body, state or condition that is the guna of tamas. Tamas is only the indication of coming into a conditioned state of being, which can be external as well as internal. When the mind is fixated on a thought, idea or perception, whether good or bad, it is the tamasic state of mind. Tamas is often defined as darkness. However, according to Samkhya, tamas does not symbolize

darkness, but a condition. The effort required to come to a state of being is the process of action, and that is rajo guna.

The building that you are looking at is in the guna of tamas right now, but when it was being constructed that was the guna of rajas, and when the building was in the planning stage on the drawing board, the guna was sattwa. Sattwa is the state of inner luminosity, rajas of inner action and tamas of inner conditioning. These three gunas intermingle in the unmanifest dimension and when a being is born, gunas come along with the basic instincts.

The three gunas are inherent in each and every object and are identified by their manifesting karma. Sri Swamiji gives the example of a knife. A knife is an object made of metal and has a wooden base. However, its application can bring forth the three qualities, gunas, of the knife or of your character. For when you hold the knife in your hand it becomes an extension of your body. A different character will manifest depending on the application of the knife. If you use it to stab and kill somebody, the use of knife is seen as tamasic. Here tamas relates to a negative quality. If you use it to perform surgery and save somebody's life, it depicts the sattwic quality, which supports and nourishes life. If you use the knife to chop vegetables to nourish your body, the rajasic nature is perceived. The knife is one single object, but when applied for a purpose, a quality manifests.

In the same manner, we receive this system, the body, mind, senses, intellect and emotions, as a gift from Purusha and Prakriti, the cosmic powers responsible for creation. As part of that gift, the three gunas have also come. The gunas intermingle, mix and merge with the four components of the operating system to create interaction of life with the world.

Manifestation of gunas

In their cosmic state the gunas are in a state of balance, but when life manifests one guna becomes predominant. Why does that happen? The cause is that the samskaras or impressions that come with us as our *prarabdha*, fixed karmas, define the prominence of a guna. This is not just a philosophical presumption, even science and psychology now acknowledge this. As a part of that indestructible Supreme Spirit, the individual spirit is also free. But when it enters the realm of Prakriti, it comes with its baggage just as you carry a bag full of things when you travel. You carry a bag when you travel from one city to another, so wouldn't the soul which is making an eternal journey carry some baggage? When you are at home you are completely free, but while travelling you need things. The baggage of the spirit consists of the five senses and the mind. Every living being has a mind; all that differentiates a human being from other beings is that it is aware of its mind due to the faculty of intelligence.

It is due to this faculty that we experience our mind, joy, sorrow, karmas and reactions. So, when the mind and spirit enter the realm of Prakriti, they are subject to the three gunas.

The three gunas are perceived in the sensory associations with sense objects. They can be perceived in the samskaras as either weakness of character or strength of character. They can be perceived in swabahava as optimism, pessimism or indifference. They can also be seen in the instincts.

Take the case of passion, for example. If sattwa predominates in passion, it will uplift the individual; if tamas predominates in passion, it will drag him down to gross dimensions; if rajas is predominant, a flirtatious nature will be seen.

In the case of craving, if tamas is predominant one becomes selfish and self-centred. If sattwa is predominant then there is no craving; there is only an understanding of the need of the craving for fulfilment and not an obsessive desire to acquire the object of craving.

Similarly, when sleep is tamasic or sattwic its quality is different. Even fears and insecurities have tamasic, sattwic and rajasic qualities. The gunas mix with the basic structures of life to give birth to a new identity, expression and experience.

If you are in a depressed, anxious or agitated frame of mind and the thoughts are negative, it indicates a conditioning of the mind which is tamasic and destructive, for yourself and for others too. If there is joy and happiness in life and the world looks bright and shiny, then that happiness and optimism is not only personal, the sattwa expression is not only personal, you also project it outwards. The gunas control and direct the senses and the mind. The expression of the predominance of the gunas is through the mind. The mood of the mind depicts the three gunas. When the mind associates with a guna, the thinking alters, the expressions alter. The gunas first manifest in the mind and then in behaviour and action.

21

Desire, action and mood

The first function of the mind is creation of desire. Without desire, the mind cannot exist. Analyze your everyday situations and you will find that behind every action there was and is a desire. Desire is the first expression of the mind, and it is self-oriented: "I wish to attain, I wish to receive, I wish to acquire, this is my need."

With desire comes action, the second stage. When the desire is clear in the mind, actions performed are aimed at obtaining the desired results. Thus, life is a play of desires and action, desire and performance. There is nothing beyond the two. From the basic to the imaginative, we desire things that are our need and that are our fantasies. Desires can be actual and also unattainable ambitions, but nevertheless they exist.

Desires indicate the mood, the state of mind according to the guna predominant in the mind at that particular time. The environment can create a stirring desire. If you walk into a nightclub, the senses will begin to sway to the beat of the music, the mind will be stimulated and to further stimulate yourself, you will head for the bar. The stimulation is the feeling of pleasantness, intoxication, letting go of hang-ups, the need to loosen up. On the other hand, if you walk into a peaceful environment your senses will become still.

By entering into the fold of an environment, the mental attitude changes, as the sensorial inputs in the brain are different. The environment plays a role in the expression of a qualitative behaviour. It creates the necessary mood for that behaviour to manifest, whether positive or destructive. In a gloomy, depressive, negative environment, one's actions will not have the clarity that one needs to have in life. The mind, thoughts and actions will become negative and lose contact with all the beautiful associations in the past. In such a state all the help that is received has no meaning. This affects performance; it affects the intellect, emotions, senses and perception. If one is optimistic and happy, that will also affect the mind, the senses and emotions. Therefore, always be happy. Always see the positive in everything because you have the ability to do so.

Most of the time people see the negative. However, just as you are able to see the negative, there is the possibility to see the positive as well. If you identify with the negative, you will distance yourself from enjoyment of life, and if you identify with the positive, you will gain a better, clearer understanding of situations. In my own guru's life, I have seen that no matter what the situation was, he always had a constructive outlook. In the worst of situations he saw the best of possibilities, how to improve that situation. That is the character which indicates that one has transcended the influence of moods, of the senses, mind and emotions.

A desire manifests in the mind and that is the beginning of karma. The desire is connected to the perception of an object and its acquisition. There is planning, a program is made and the person prepares to follow it. However, if a different guna is dominant in the mind, that effort is washed

away because the nature of karma changes. If someone is having a bad day, even if you give him the simplest of tasks he will mess it up. But if the head is clear and at peace the most complicated task will be accomplished dexterously. When the guna and mind join, a mood is created, and when a karma is added to this, it will be performed according to the mood.

Fruits of karma

When the gunas combine with the operating system of life, they manifest in the form of actions and give three different kinds of results. The action which comes with the positive quality of sattwa will give a positive result. The action which comes with the negative quality of tamas will bring forth a negative result. And the third is *mishrit*, mixed result – it can go both ways, towards upliftment or towards suppression.

We only aspire for the good, but we don't know how to be good. For us, 'being good' means doing the right thing externally, but in yoga being good means doing the right thing inside the mind. If the mind is doing the right thing, then the external performance will also be right. Exponents of karma yoga say that one should strive for the completion of an action, each action being a creative one, done with perfection, and there should be no expectation of a result. However, if you look at the realities of life, no one is evolved enough to deny the results, the fruits of action.

Whenever there is any action, there is a natural craving for a better outcome or result. Even while it is said not to expect results, just keep on doing your duty, in reality we are all expecting results. It is one thing for Lord Krishna to say in the *Bhagavad Gita* that you have the right to perform karma but you do not have the right to its result. But as an individual you cannot make that statement – with what authority do you say it? Have you lived what you believed in? A human being expects results, even a spiritual aspirant expects results. If one does japa, one wants to have an experience; if one practises meditation, one wants darshan.

You have expectations in your own life, but tell others to live without expectation of results, because it is written in the *Gita*, it is what the gurus and teachers say. Every being expects results. In the normal human state, every individual expects results.

It is not wrong to expect results. The only thing that is wrong is the hankering for and obsession with the result. When we are obsessed suffering and pleasure both come. When pleasure comes, we are attracted towards that which is pleasurable. *Sukhanushayi ragah* – we are attracted to those conditions, situations and objects through which we can experience happiness and pleasure. That is called *raga* or attraction. Alternatively, we feel aversion, *dwesha*, towards conditions which cause suffering; we don't want to suffer because we are fearful of suffering. *Dukhanushayi dweshah* – there is rejection of the conditions which cause suffering. So the hankering is for the result from which we feel pleased, because we believe it will make us happy, and if the result is seen as displeasing, we avoid it.

One has to accept success and failure both. Often when one fails, one says it was the will of God and when one succeeds one says it was ones own doing. To speak of your success as your doing and achievement indicates a tamasic frame of mind. And, when you say you failed because of God's will, you are indicating a non-understanding, tamasic condition of life, as you are not willing to take on the responsibility for your actions. So accept both. Just as we accept day and night as natural events of life, success and failure are also natural events of living.

Have the expectation of a benevolent, auspicious and fruitful result, but don't hanker after it, don't get obsessed about it. If you get obsessed you lose your creativity, your awareness and acquire tunnel vision. If you try to look at the world through a pipe, your vision will be limited. That is tunnel vision. In obsession, the mind focuses only on one thing. In depression people think gloomily; in elation, they think only of happiness. All these indicate tunnel vision.

When you perform a karma, do it well. Whatever you have to get in return, you will get. If you drink water, your thirst is bound to be quenched. You don't drink a bucket of water, one glass suffices. The circumstances come and go, expectations are always there in one form or another. For my life I wish to be able to walk the path that I have been guided to walk. That is the expectation of a result from myself. What needs to be handled is attachment to a result. Go on performing your karmas with awareness and do not pay attention to gains and losses. When you are able to balance yourself between gain and loss, that will be the highest balance of life. Sri Krishna said in the *Bhagavad Gita* (2:47):

Siddhyasiddhyoh samo bhootwaa samatvam yoga uchyate.

Balanced in success and failure, evenness of mind is called yoga.

Whether you succeed or fail in your effort, assume the attitude of a witness and allow the state of samatvam, equanimity, to come into your life. That state has been called yoga. When the mind is balanced and contented, you feel happy. Free yourself from identifying with success and failure. Continue to have the expectation for results, but do not be obsessed with or without them. When you expect a result, it becomes a goal for you. If I want to become a good sannyasin, I am expecting results, however this expectation becomes the goal and purpose of life which enables me to make effort. If I renounce that expectation and say, "Whatever has to happen will happen", I will never be able to walk the path. There will be too many diversions. So, whoever comes into this world should walk with an expectation, and success or failure should not deviate them.

The middle path

The spiritual traditions say, keep to the middle path. Buddha advocated the middle path. He said, don't be a rightist, don't be a leftist (not in the political sense), but walk the middle path. Don't walk on the right side of the road or on the left side; be in the middle from where you can see both sides.

The Upanishads have defined this middle path as being as sharp as the razor's edge. You have to tread carefully as, with a little slip, you will bleed to death. This happens in life too. If you slip from your focus and are distracted, the journey stops there. The intentions and motivations stagnate at that point and you can't move forward. Where you slip, o the left or to the right, is where your journey ends. However, if you keep on walking carefully with awareness, maintaining your balance, equilibrium and equipoise, then you can cover the distance of the journey. Therefore, equipoise, samatvam, is the highest quality of human life. When equipoise becomes a powerful manifesting quality in life, then harmony sets in where one is not affected by desires and there is no hankering, craving or obsession for a result.

What this means is that one has to change the conditioning of the mind. Even as a baby, we hanker for things, as a child and as a young adult we desire other things. As we grow up, we view the world differently. As we gain more experience, we understand the world in a different light. There is a process of maturity.

In each state, each condition of life, one needs to understand that particular condition, that particular desire and that particular need for the fulfilment of the expectation. The hankering for fulfilment is the cause of happiness or suffering, causing a self-oriented awareness. People are so self-oriented that many times they reject and hide from their own weaknesses as well as their own light.

If there is anything that a human being is afraid of in this world, it is their own luminosity. All desire luminosity, but when confronted with luminosity they say, "Enough." It happened to Arjuna. He said to Krishna on the battlefield, "Show me your cosmic form." When Krishna showed him the cosmic form, Arjuna said, "Please come back to your normal form, I like that one better. I can identify with that. I can't identify with your cosmic form, I can't identify with your luminosity. I can identify with you when I see you as myself."

The gunas associate with karmas and give birth to the experience of joy and sorrow. We associate joy and sorrow with success and failure. To find a balance between the two is yoga. If there is inner balance in success and failure of karmas, it is karma yoga. If there is inner balance in the success and failure of the intellect, it is jnana yoga. If there is inner balance in the emotions that flow towards desires and aspire to flow towards God, that is the beginning of bhakti yoga, and if you apply the principle of balance to your body, you will be able to master hatha yoga. Balance is a state of mind; it is not a practice of yoga. Therefore, the first yogic sadhana should be acquiring balance, harmony, equanimity. Asana and pranayama are physical practices. The internal sadhana should be the effort to achieve equanimity. You can do this through japa, mantra, observation of the mind, pratyahara, dharana, dhyana, kundalini yoga, kriya yoga – there are many practices. These are all methods, but there comes a time when we achieve the knowledge and attach our karma to yoga.

For karma yoga, you have to understand the mind, gunas, moods, joy and sorrow. Sri Swamiji says that one performs karma yoga to achieve immunity from the reactive conditions of mind. Remain free of the reactions that arise in the mind due to different situations. A negative emotional reaction causes you suffering, so do not become emotional even as you undergo the suffering. As soon as you become emotional the mood changes and you will lose your clarity and enter into darkness. But if you can maintain balance then the mood will not change and you will be able to change the situation. If someone slaps you, you will be able to prove that they were wrong and they will also accept it, but if you slap him back you will only end up in a scuffle and whoever is stronger will win. So, ultimately the emotional responses, mental responses and sensory responses have to be managed to convert karma into yoga.

After acquiring balance one frees oneself from the desire to experience pleasure and thereby also becomes free of the experience of sorrow. Whatever be the result of karma, it does not matter because you cannot control the result. Of course, if you perform a negative karma you will get a negative response and if you perform a positive karma you will reap a positive response.

The experience of life

People define karma as the law of action and reaction. The law of action and reaction is the inherent nature of things. If you bring both hands together, there is bound to be a sound. Bringing the two hands together can be construed as action and the creation of sound as the reaction. Action and reaction is your expression.

Karma is not the law of action and reaction to which you are subject; rather, karma is life. The experiences of life are

karma and the knowledge of the experiences of life is jnana. This is the difference between the two. As far as reaction and action are concerned, remember that every potential cause has a potential effect inherent in it. Every cause has an effect hidden in it just as shadow is hidden in the body. Shadow is part of the body, it is formed from the body, but to see it you have to be in sunlight. Thus a cause has an inherent effect and that is karma. Action and reaction are not karmas; they are karmic behaviours. Every cause has an effect hidden in it. This body is the cause, this mind is the cause, and the effect is hidden in the body and the mind. That is the expectation, the desire, the craving.

Managing karma

The spiritual traditions say, "Improve your karma." What do they mean?

To manage the karma, one needs to know the basic operating systems of life and understand which software is predominant amongst them. In the life of every individual one vritti is more predominant than others. I have no fears in life, I have no obsessive passions in life, I don't have much craving. In my case my problem has been the nidra vritti, sleep. In the early days when I would go to sleep at night, my guru brothers would pick up the whole bed and leave it outside the gates of the ashram. I would be completely unaware of what was happening. On waking I would find myself outside the gates! Sleep was my weakness. My guru used my weakness to train me. He educated me in my sleep, in yoga nidra. He used my weakness and converted it into a strength.

As far as the timing for waking up was concerned, I had to work on that. So I observed my sleeping pattern for some time. At first, in the attempt to change it, I set the alarm clock for four in the morning and said that from tomorrow I will get up at four o'clock. I did that for two days, and on the third day I did not hear the alarm! The same happened on the fourth day.

I said to myself, this is not going to work. Sleep is going to make me tamasic, lethargic, dull and lazy. What do I do to rectify this? This time I set the alarm at 6.50 for one week, ten minutes early. Then at 6.40 for another week. Then 6.30, 6.20, 6.10 . . . until I came to 4 o'clock over a period of a few months. The conditioning was gradual, it was not based on a rigid determination to do it from tomorrow. I realized that I could not fulfil such a decision because the mind was not prepared, it was weak. If it was strong in the first place I would not have had the problem. I could not rectify the weakness with direct confrontation with my vritti so I had to use a trick to change the habit of the mind – I just shifted the hands of the alarm by a few minutes every day. Thus the progression was smooth. I came to a point where I had to train my mind. Had I used any other method I would never have been able to train myself. I would have been struggling with that vritti which was creating a negative condition in my mind. Some training had to take place.

This is how the basic components of life have to be fine-tuned. Some people have a predominance of craving in their life, every five minutes they go to the refrigerator. They don't know what to do with their inner craving, so they try to fulfil it through food. It is a psychological response to an inner craving which they can't understand. If they understood it they wouldn't head for the fridge. When craving is not consciously known but is desired, it manifests as attraction for food. Food represents nourishment, the craving is to be nourished somehow or the other. Even if it is a mental craving, it is nourished by eating food.

Craving can also be emotional and sensual. Those who are habitually promiscuous for example, their craving is passion – the need to experiment and connect. Psychoanalysts call it the psychology of youth. But the fact is that when you start chasing passion the mind gets disturbed, as passion is an obsession. It is a bondage; it is not a liberating power. It is intended for personal gratification, so its fulfilment only

31

increases it and binds one so that one loses touch with the appropriate qualities and positive conditions of life. The physiological and psychological effects of passion are felt just as the physiological and psychological effects of craving and sleep are felt. Too much sleep is bad and sleep deprivation is bad. Too much passion is bad and passion deprivation is bad. Therefore, an understanding of the operating systems of life through contemplation and meditation helps to manage the karmas of life.

Karma and rebirth

Karmas are acquired from the past and also created in the present. The eastern systems believe in rebirth. Semitic religions do not believe in rebirth officially, although even Jesus Christ spoke on reincarnation. He said that his guru, John the Baptist, was an incarnation of Elijah. Christ recognized rebirth. The Church is an institution, and I am not talking of institutions. I am talking of the experience a person can have. Christ had that and he spoke about it.

The scriptures have also spoken about reincarnation. Sages and swamis have spoken about it and even present-day scientists are discussing and researching it. The eastern philosophies maintain that if what we accumulate in this life, the impressions we gather, are not worked through and not released in this life, they are carried forward into the next. It is like writing a word with a pencil on a blank piece of paper. You can erase the word, but the impression of the pencil will remain on the paper, the force which you have applied will be seen in the form of the script even though the visible marks do not exist any more. What you write can never be completely erased from the paper. The visual component can be erased, but not that which has imprinted itself on the paper. That is the karma that you come with. The mind does not die. If the mind was different how would memory of the past be retained? The present mind is not different from the past mind. I do not get your mind in my next life; I get my own mind in my next life.

We take birth again and again only to experience and exhaust karma. Prakriti tries to attract the spirit towards matter, and the spirit, due to its inherent nature, wants to go towards God. When the spirit assumes a material body with the help of Prakriti, it needs the senses and the mind, but when it makes the effort to unite with God it does not need the senses or the mind as this effort is not external, intellectual or conscious. If you light a fire, the flames will travel upwards. A tree will also always grow skywards. Similarly, the energies of the mind always try to rise upwards, but we pull them down due to the influences of karma.

The impressions that come as a package with us in this life are called *prarabdha*; they are the invisible script on the paper that cannot be seen but influences our lives. They are connected with the gunas. That is how the game in life begins. We take birth, play as a child, receive education, stabilize ourselves professionally, but while we are playing this game, according to our prarabdha, the prominence of the guna and the basic instincts, a mentality is formed, which is described as our character or personality.

The search for happiness

After acquiring a body and mind, what is it that one looks for? Happiness. That is the law of life; a child looks for happiness as much as an old person. The main struggle in life is to be free of suffering and discover happiness. You make all efforts to experience happiness. However, the present mental make-up does not correspond to the experience of happiness, for happiness is the state of *ananda*, bliss. That state of bliss is experienced only by a mind which is not under bondage.

When the mind is not free, you may get a glimpse of happiness but you will not be able to stabilize its experience. That glimpse will be followed by sorrow. The times when one feels happy, the mind is completely free. Look at your own life. When you are happy how elated you feel, the whole world shines, the mind feels light, the body feels light, you are riding on high waves. That is the experience of freedom, liberation. When sorrow appears, it feels as if there is a mountain load on top, one feels tied down to the experience of narrowness and restlessness. So, the meaning of *moksha*, liberation, is freedom from sorrow. It means to free up that which is bound. What is the bondage that ties you down – it is not the senses, it is not the mind. The senses and the mind are always there. One can be free of the results, the circumstances which take away the state of happiness, and these are the sorrows – the afflictions, ignorance and fear of death.

Karmas are connected to these joys and sorrows. The gunas and the instincts are affected by joy and sorrow. Even a tamasic person will experience sattwa, peace and bliss when there is happiness in life. And a sattwic person will experience tamasic conditions due to suffering. Therefore, the aim of the karma in this world is the acquisition of happiness through different means.

God thought of happiness and sorrow, and Prakriti has implanted them in our nature. Joy makes one weak, while suffering awakens the tendency of *purushartha*, self-effort. Those who run after happiness remain weak, but those who endure suffering acquire strength of mind. All the finest achievements in the world have taken place due to confrontation with suffering, not due to pleasure. If Siddhartha hadn't seen human suffering, he would not have become Buddha. Therefore, the sages say, make suffering the basis of your evolution. The inclination for exertion that will awaken in you, the sattwa that you will acquire through it, is unparalleled.

Kunti said the same thing to Krishna at the end of the Mahabharata war. The great war was over, Yudhishthira had been crowned king, there was prosperity and peace in the kingdom. Krishna decided to go back to his kingdom. He bid farewell to everyone, but when he came to Kunti, she said to him, "Now that we have peace and prosperity, you are leaving. But when we were in sorrow you would appear before us at the very thought of you. I wish that there always be suffering in our lives so we can remember you and be in your presence." Only Kunti has made such a wish in history – "God, give us sorrow because that is when you are present with us. When you give us happiness, we are separated from you."

Who goes towards spirituality, to God and to saints and sages? Only one who is unhappy. Suffering brings us closer to God. Joy and sorrow are due to Prakriti, not due to God. God does not want us to be happy or unhappy; He wants us to be content in whatever condition or place we are in. Prakriti manifests as yoga and maya and brings forth both joy and sorrow. One who achieves the end of desires receives *jnana*, knowledge. The rest continue to struggle with pain and pleasure. Many come to spirituality in search of joy, that's all right. You should experience joy and happiness, but don't forget the aim of your life. The aim of life is to free yourself from bondages so you can experience total freedom.

In the realm of Prakriti, due to gunas one experiences joy and sorrow. If tamas predominates, one goes towards pleasure, if sattwa is predominant one will go beyond the senses, manas, buddhi, chitta and ahamkara. When a tamas-dominant person performs karma, they tie themselves up in knots, when a sattwa-dominant person performs karma, they free themselves of knots, and a rajas-dominant person gets mixed results.

In the ashram, you perform the same tasks as at home – cooking, cleaning, working, sweeping, thinking. There is no difference in the method of work but in your understanding and knowledge. Through the environment that exists in the ashram, through *satsang*, association with the wise, *sadhana*, spiritual practice, *shraddha*, faith, and *samarpan*, surrender, one acquires the understanding of what is useful and what is not, and what is appropriate and what is not. While performing the same tasks at home, one does not get such clear understanding. In the ashram you get the stick of the guru; at home there is no one to hit you on the head. When you are hit by the guru, you awaken a little, you think about whether what you are doing is right or wrong, you acquire an awareness of yourself and slowly the *drashta*, witness, attitude develops. This is not achieved in one day, but once the process starts one gradually become the witness of karmas and thoughts. This is the meaning of spiritual learning.

Plant the seed, prune the tree

If you plant a seed, it will germinate. And when the fruits appear ten years later you will see the result of what you had planted. This applies even in spiritual life. Therefore, don't be in a hurry, be patient. Don't expect to have a transcendental experience in one week of meditation. Plant the seed of meditation and protect it, nurture it, nourish it, take care of it and you will receive the fruits of meditation ten years down the line. It won't happen in one week and don't expect it either. Nature follows its own course of law. Human effort in life should be to provide the right condition, environment and the right seed to flower.

We are all life members of the club called earth and when we depart from this body the membership will end.

Until then we are all life members of human society. Therefore, the quality of karma has to be transformed from negative, limiting and destructive to creative and uplifting. By observation of the instincts, doing the appropriate action at the appropriate time, by improving the swabahava, one can transform the karmas.

How to improve one's character, swabhava? If you don't interfere with the growth of a tree, the branches will sprout and grow in all directions. If you want to ensure that the tree grows straight, you have to start pruning and trimming right from the beginning. Do that to your life. You have never pruned the tree of your life. One crooked branch goes down in one direction, another goes crooked in another direction. You show the gardener the tree with all the crooked branches and say, "I wish the tree was straight!" The gardener says, "I will have to use a saw to cut the crooked branches." And you say, "No, you can't use a saw, it hurts, it is painful." The gardener says, "There is no option."

In life we fail to realize the importance of right living. If one lives in the right manner with proper trimming and pruning from the beginning, trimming our samskaras, our nature, our behaviour, then after the initial effort the tree will automatically grow straight.

Necessity of sadhana
The trimming happens through yoga sadhana. Yoga sadhana means working on the human nature and you have to do that much yourself. Spiritual life exposes one to the limited side of ones nature. That is what you see in meditation. When you see that limited aspect of yourself, there is fear or the feeling of guilt. We go through mental crises when we try to manage, alter and transform a condition which we have lived with for so many years. When the trimming is not done initially, the twigs become big, hard, strong branches, then rectification is impossible.

Just as we prune and trim a tree to ensure its proper growth, we have to trim our nature by cultivating a different attitude to the present one. Is the glass half full or half empty? Which attitude do you express? If you are aware of the absences in life you will say that it is half empty and if you are aware of the gains in life, you will say it is half full. The attitude is different. This positive attitude is the result of the association of your mind with your wisdom, knowledge and understanding.

Transformation

When the mind associates with knowledge, with jnana, the attitude changes. When the mind is connected to the senses, the response is different. When the mind is connected to a desire, the response is different and when it is connected to jnana, the response is different.

The transformation of character happens through observation, understanding, knowledge and awareness. Understanding and awareness equals wisdom. Understanding without awareness is only understanding, but understanding plus awareness equals wisdom. It is through wisdom that one can manage the trimming of character. Instincts are managed through meditation, and swabhava through trimming, awareness and understanding.

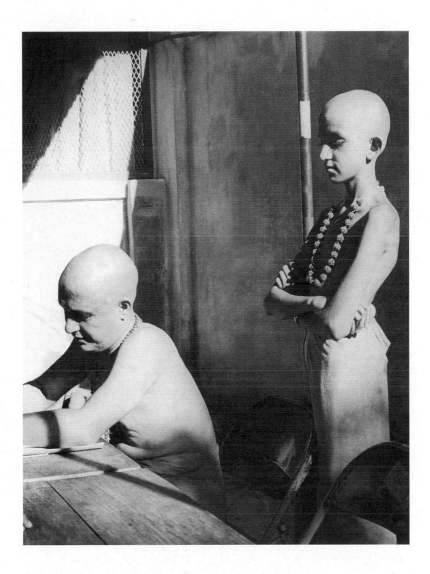

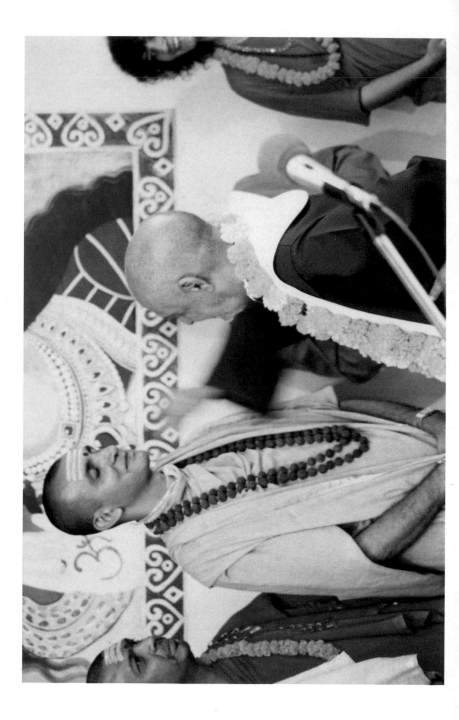

Operating System and Mind

27th February 2010

Our life is experienced through four components:
1. the basic instincts – ahara, nidra, bhaya, maithuna
2. our essential nature
3. impressions
4. sense perceptions.

Together these constitute the primary operating software of our life. The gunas – sattwa, rajas and tamas – emerge to support them, and when the gunas mix with the software, there is a change in its performance.

Management of instincts

In order to practise karma yoga, one has to begin with management of the operating system of life. This is achieved by associating with jnana. For example, you are walking on a road in the dark and spot a piece of rope. The thought comes, "It is a snake!" When you believe that the object on the road is a snake, you will never think of it as a rope. As you identify that object as a snake, the corresponding responses will emerge: fear, palpitation, nervousness, the desire to flee. At that moment, if somebody were to tell you that it is a piece of rope, your response would change. The moment you understand that it is a piece of rope and not a snake, the fear leaves you, your heartbeat becomes normal, the desire to flee dissipates. In this manner, through knowledge, through understanding, you can overcome one component of the instincts, fear.

The difficulty in the management of instincts is to connect them with awareness. *Kamaturanam na bhayam na lajja* – "When passion is raging, there is no inhibition, no shame, no fear." The passionate obsession and the lack of awareness of the instinct bypass all restrictions, norms and limitations. When you experience the power of the different instincts, at that particular time you respond to that particular instinct. No one is aware of this process; no one is analyzing this process. The first component in the yogic management of instincts, whether craving, sleep, fear or sensuality, is awareness – to know that it exists.

The second is analysis. Think: is my awareness and understanding appropriate or not? Is what I imagined like the scenario of the piece of rope that was believed to be a snake, or can I through some means shed some light and see the real thing? Analysis is the second component in the management of instincts.

The third is restraint. Control the reactions, control the responses, don't overreact, restrain yourself – to allow the analysis to take place and the awareness to be nurtured. Once analysis has been undertaken and awareness has been nurtured, then one can tell whether the response is appropriate or not. That natural response is based on *sanyam*, restraint.

The fourth modification of the instincts is through wisdom, *jnana*. Through analysis, you understand the proper-improper aspect of the instinct. Then convert that understanding into a positive force, with wisdom. So, the four methods are: awareness, analysis, restraint and wisdom.

Management of swabhava

Next is management of *swabhava*, character or nature. Human nature and character are based on different impressions and qualities that we inherit and awaken in our life. We inherit certain impressions and qualities at the time of birth. They define the character and the personality.

A person can be optimistic or pessimistic, a person can have faith or be a fatalist. One can be positive with happiness

and joy in life or one can be pessimistic, always feeling hopeless. Such behaviours of the personality are not external impositions but expressions of the inherent qualities which manifest in the course of life.

How can one transform this character when in the conditioned state of life, mind and the senses, all the energies are flowing outwards towards sense objects? Our present awareness is external; it is material, sensorial and sensual. Thus the projections and swabhava are externalized, which causes the negative and limiting tendencies to raise their head in the form of jealousy, frustration, depression, hatred, lust, greed, the desire to possess. At the core of all these manifestations is the basic need to satisfy our own nature.

After all, why do we feel envious or jealous of somebody? The feeling is that the other person is getting more than me, whether it be more attention, more affection, more consideration, more wealth or more happiness. When we see fulfilment in another person's life and the lack of it in our own, then jealousy raises its head. Comparison between two people is the cause of jealousy – me and you. If you do not compare yourself to me, if I do not compare myself to you, there is no cause for jealousy. It is the same with hatred, love or anger.

Remember that two separate things have to come together in order to create the third. The two things here are 'sad little me' and 'happy you'. When you begin to identify yourself with sad little me and perceive the other person as the one who is happy, then, at that time the negative traits of human nature come to surface in the form of greed, envy, jealousy and so on. They alter the mental perception, cover the light of wisdom and understanding with *avidya*, ignorance, and you become dull. That is swabhava.

How does one manage the negative states, the destructive and limiting states of one's own nature? Through cultivation of positive qualities in life. The modification of swabhava is a sadhana. If you are jealous of someone, what is the antidote to that jealousy? Discover it and apply that in life to manage jealousy. If there is frustration, what is the antidote for frustration, not external but your own? Discover that and apply it to overcome frustration. Hatred – find the antidote in a positive manner and you will be able to manage that tendency.

Swabhava, the character and nature, has to be managed by complimenting the negative with the positive, the restrictive with the creative. Do not try to pull out the negative from your nature. That is a part of your nature, you cannot pull it out. It has been with you in the genes of your mind from birth. In the mental genetic structure, not the physical, the DNA of all these experiences exists. The genes of negativity exist, the genes of hatred, lust and anger exist. You cannot modify, remove or destroy them because if you do so you are destroying yourself. However, you can manage them by cultivating the positive strength to overcome the negative weakness. That is known as conversion, converting the negative power into a positive strength.

Management of samskaras

How do we manage samskaras, the third software? A samskara has to be first understood through a meditative process. The meditative learning starts with pratyahara and dharana. An aspirant can only go up to dharana, not beyond. Dhyana is an experience out of the reach of every individual. As a human being one can go up to dharana, not beyond. After one has overcome the physical identity one can experience dhyana.

Once I was travelling in Tasmania in 1977 in a car with a driver. We were going through the countryside. There was a lake and beside the water a massive willow tree was growing. I looked up at that willow tree and the car moved on. At that moment something shifted in my head. I lost my body awareness and became the tree while I was in the car. It was a frightening experience! That was *dhyana*, meditation. Meditation is a frightening experience, as when you lose awareness of the body what is there to hold on to? I had become the tree. I could feel the sensation of ants and insects crawling up the bark of the trunk. I could feel the wind blowing through the leaves and the swaying of the twigs and branches in the breeze. I could feel the water lapping the roots of the tree. The experience lasted only a few moments, but it felt like hours. The mind totally lost physical perception of myself as an individual and became the tree. That is the state of meditation. Meditation cannot be practised; it is a state of mind, it is absolute identification with the object of meditation which you acquire after you have perfected *dharana*, concentration.

Sri Swamiji rarely used the word meditation or dhyana; he said concentration. Our limited mind can go only that far. How fast can you run? According to the limits of your legs and the stamina of your body, maybe three, four or six kilometres per hour. Your body is incapable of running beyond that speed. Just as there are physical limitations in running, there are mental limitations in concentration, which do not allow meditation to take place. As an aspirant you can only go up to dharana. Human beings till today in history have never reached the state of meditation. All the aspirants have come to the point of dharana, total concentration and focus. After that the body has to be transcended, the senses have to be transcended in order to come to the meditative state. Therefore, although I am using the word meditation, it should not be taken in the sense of higher meditation, but only the lower meditation where you develop and cultivate the awareness of your inner behaviour, your inner personality.

You have to undergo a process upon initiating your meditative discovery, in which you develop and cultivate the awareness of psyche and emotions, and that is the system of pratyahara and dharana. Those who do not go through these stages of pratyahara and dharana cannot understand the theory, philosophy and experience of meditation. Just as in present day and time samadhi is out of reach of every person, meditation is also out of reach of every person. However, through concentration, through focusing the externalized mind you can discover and realize your own psyche.

The deeper mind is like a picture book. On each page there is a picture, but to look at the picture you have to turn the page. In the same manner, deep inside the human psyche are the impressions from all previous lifetimes rubber-stamped on each page. It is like your passport. Your passport contains the information of the journeys gone through in the valid period of the passport and the old passports contain information of the journeys undertaken in the past and they have those immigration stamps. You use the new passport for your travels and also retain the old passports.

The old passports are the past impressions and the new passport is what you are living at present. The old passports indicate that these are the countries you have journeyed to, which is confirmed by the stamp of immigration. When you open an old passport and see that many years ago you had gone to Egypt, the memories of that journey will come. In life, you open the psyche, discover the immigration stamp of a karma, a samskara and realize that. First you have to discover it and that is achieved through dhyana, a meditative process through which we can go deep into our own nature. The practice of mantra helps in that.

Mantra is a powerful tool to stop the diversions and distractions of the mind. However, practising mantra properly is a difficult process. I was initiated in mantra in 1966. Sri Swamiji was sitting on the steps of the sadhana hall in the old Sivananda Ashram and he called me and said, "Sit down." Then he said, "Repeat this mantra after me." That was my mantra initiation. He spoke it once and I repeated it once. But then I forgot it. I did not have the courage to go to Sri Swamiji and say, "Can you please remind me of my mantra." So I kept quiet. After many months, one day I was sitting quietly, the body relaxed . . . and suddenly the mantra flashed in my mind and I started repeating it. I realized that this was the mantra given to me! I was so happy that I ran to Sri Swamiji and said, "Swamiji, I am doing my mantra sadhana." The mantra memory suddenly came. I had forgotten it. The power of the mantra given by my guru was such that it was active in my unconscious mind.

I asked Sri Swamiji how many malas of mantra I should practise. He said, "Only one mala with awareness." Till today I am trying to complete that one full mala with awareness. If I only have to move the beads and chant the mantra, I can do many malas in one hour. If I have to be aware of each mantra 108 times over, I don't know where the mind goes after the fiftieth. Then I realize that my mind is not fixed on the mantra. So I again drag it back and start the mala from number one. Till today I have not been able to complete one mala of mantra.

Management of the senses

The management of the fourth component of the operating system, the *indriyas*, the senses, is done by refocusing their attention.

If the eyes look at something or someone and find it desirable – a pleasing flower or a desirable person, at that time one should observe one's thoughts. You should look at that object, the flower, and say, "What a wonderful shape, colour, form, beauty, smell. Up to that point it is fine but then alertness has to come in. What is the next stage after appreciating the beauty of the flower? What do you want to do after appreciation of the beauty?

You have to refocus your attention by telling yourself, "It is not my need, it is only my infatuation, nothing more than that." Infatuation is different from need. Learn to

46

differentiate between the two. When you are able to do that you can have control of the senses, *indriya sanyam*. Then the mind will not follow the senses, the emotions will not follow the senses, you will not follow the senses. You will be able to manage them, guide them, redirect them, refocus them to develop a positive response, a constructive response.

These are the ways in which you can manage the four basic components of the operating system.

Permutation and combination

The combination of the human operating systems – the primary operating system; instincts, nature, impressions, sense perceptions – and the secondary operating system, the gunas, give birth to a third behaviour.

Imagine a glass of crystal clear water and a bottle of black ink. These are two separate things, different and distinct. Let us say that the crystal clear water is operating system number one and the black ink is operating system number two, the gunas. One drop of black in the crystal clear water will darken the clarity of water. The clarity will no longer be seen, instead, the blackness will be seen. The essential nature of water has changed and a third, mutated form has emerged because of the combination of two things. This is called *vikara*, modification.

The same analogy applies to the gunas. Presume that the colour of tamas is black, rajas is red and sattwa is white. When a drop of any of these colours falls into the clear water of the instincts, nature, impressions or sense perceptions, that colour will become visible in these four. So, when the gunas, the support system, and the basic operating system intermingle with each other, a third experience emerges, and that is of the mind, the antahkaran.

Whatever changes take place due to the mixing of the gunas and the software, their effect is produced in the mind. The expression or emergence of this third experience takes place in the mind. When the gunas mix with the instincts a vibration emerges in the mind. If the two are separate and there is no permutation and combination, no vibration will arise. The expression and experience of the mind emerges only when there is a vikara. Observe your own mind: when do you become aware of it? When there is an activity in the thoughts, desires or ambitions. If the mind is quiet and at peace, then your attention is not drawn to it, you don't experience it. You know that the mind exists, but you are aware of it only when there is a disturbance in its natural state. A problem, worry or desire becomes the medium to experience the mind. Until a tendency arises in the mind, one does not feel the mind. This mind is the kitchen of life. Everything is cooked in the mind.

The kitchen of life

The mind is the kitchen of life. And there are pots and pans too in the mind. The mind has four components: manas, chitta, buddhi and ahamkara. *Manas* is the reasoning mind; *buddhi* is the intelligence; *chitta*, the memories; *ahamkara*, the ego identity. The ego, ahamkara, is the pot, the cauldron of this kitchen. Chitta, the memories, are water which is filled in the cauldron. Buddhi, the intellect, is spice. And manas is vegetables and rice and bread. In manas you chop up the vegetables. Buddhi sprinkles the vegetables of the manas with condiments, gives it a taste. Then you put the vegetables in the water of chitta and it is cooked in the cauldron of ahamkara.

The mind is our kitchen, where food is cooked. For this we take different items from different aspects of our nature; one ambition from here, one desire from there, one action from here, one memory from there, one understanding from here, one need from there. We mix it all up and say, "I have decided that I want to achieve this in life." That means that your food is cooked.

When the food is cooked in the mind, one becomes aware of the feeling, guna or desire that is being cooked. Normally one may know about the existence of the three gunas, but may not be aware of which one is predominant.

This is a reason why no one is aware of their basic nature, for it is subtle, hidden and invisible, but it exists. The gunas are subtle, unmanifest and invisible, but they exist. When the food is cooked we become aware of what we want and do not want. The mind takes ingredients from the operating systems and support systems to create a desire, for its own fulfilment and preservation.

The nature of desire
Everyone is troubled in life due to the khitchadi cooked in the mind. Whether it be jealousy, hatred, anger, greed, attachment, deceit, love, compassion – all these internal experiences, whether good or bad, right or wrong, are cooked and experienced in the mind. These experiences don't come alone, they are always associated with another object, subject,

person, ambition, mentality or thought. Anger is not born alone; it is connected with a subject, object, person or environment. Fear is not born alone; it is connected with a subject, object, person or environment. There is no element which manifests independently in our life, and its manifestation always has a cause, a basis, a medium. That cause is the inherent desire.

All desires are for two things: self-fulfilment and self-preservation. "Nothing should harm me, I should always be happy. My needs have to be fulfilled, my aspirations have to be fulfilled." Everything is in relation to oneself. Such behaviour is seen in material as well as spiritual life. Ask the sannyasins sitting here what their aspirations are. Their aspirations are for themselves. Ask a sannyasin like Swami Satyananda what does he desire. He will say, "For them, not for me." That is the difference.

I am not denying the need for fulfilment and self-preservation; it should be there, but without obsession. What will you do with a hundred chocolates? You need only one, give the other ninety-nine to others who will be grateful and happy to receive them. If you eat all hundred, then suffer the consequences!

The scriptures say that desire is like a virgin girl who is forever pregnant. What this means is that even before a desire is born, it contains within it another desire which is ready to come out. How many children can one bear at the same time! It is so difficult to handle one pregnancy, imagine if there were thousands! When a desire emerges it is never to give joy. You think that you will find joy through the fulfilment of a desire, a wish or an ambition – but desire cannot give happiness, this has been stated by the wise. The joy that we get through desire-fulfilment is transitory, and it is gross satiation, nothing else. It is transitory because the moment it is fulfilled another desire emerges and the mind is diverted there. You begin your effort for the second even before you've enjoyed the fulfilment of the first. Therefore, the experience of joy is fleeting, and one is always attracted towards that which is fleeting and tries to possess it. If you discover a good sweet shop in a city, every time you visit it you will go to that shop, and on your second visit you will want to take some home too. That's how desire is born. The pleasure of eating was momentary, but the thought of going to that shop always stays with you.

Once someone asked a sadhu, "How to know whether I am progressing in spiritual life?" The sadhu replied, "Know that you are progressing spiritually when your desires reduce." If your desires are on the rise, know that you are going downhill. Every spiritual aspirant has this question in mind, and they think that the measure of spiritual progress is internal experiences. People believe that if they see gods and goddesses in their meditation, they are on the right track, if they see demons they are on the wrong track. If they develop a positive attitude, they are on the right track; if a negative attitude becomes strong they are on the wrong track. However, according to the wise, the vision of gods and demons is not the measure of our growth or fall. We can visualize everything in the mind; we can forget ourselves through hypnosis. That's not a big deal. Progress in life is realized when there is a reduction in desires and ambitions. Reduction means that one is not obsessed about a desire, one doesn't run after it, one doesn't lose one's balance due to it. When you lose balance of mind, you enter into a tamasic state of mind.

The main job of the mind is *manana*, contemplation. The word *mana*, mind, is derived from manana. Manana means to hold one thought and go to its roots, to hold a perception and go to its roots. This task is performed by the mind. When one loses one's balance, contemplation turns into worry and stress, chintan into chinta.

Lower mind and higher mind
The mind is of two types, the lower mind and the higher mind. We could also call them the involved mind and the discriminative mind; the gross mind and the transcendental

mind; *apara* mind and *para* mind. One is the expansive, transcendental awareness which contains everything, and the other is that in which the gross aspects of manas, buddhi, chitta and ahamkara are experienced.

At the lower level of mental behaviour, the mind is only waiting for personal gratification. This applies to all four aspects of the mind. For example, the gross buddhi or intellect connects one with the world, desires and needs, and the higher intellect allows one to have a broader perspective of life. When the intellect is only limited to 'me', it takes on a selfish quality, but in higher intelligence the selfish qualities, self-oriented desires and needs are

transcended. The intellect that we use in our daily life to study, work and live is the lower form of intelligence, and when we free ourselves from the results of this intelligence, from the notions of joy and sorrow, desire and desirelessness, right and wrong, and reach beyond this gross intelligence, then one experiences the higher intelligence, which is an expansive knowledge. There is awareness of everything, one knows and understands the working, basis and purpose of everything, every karma. But while the intellect is in the lower realm, it goes on traversing the fields of *pramana*, proof, *viparyaya*, misconception and *vikalpa*, unfounded belief.

Think about your own intellect, which you use every day, compare its manifestation or expression, and you will get an idea. This intellect is always looking for proof, making a presumption or manifesting a false knowledge in the mind. False knowledge is like the case where three people see a chameleon at different times, and describe its colour as yellow, red or black according to what they see. But one who knows the nature of a chameleon will know that this animal always changes its colour. The intellect that one uses in the world, in sense experiences, is apara buddhi. Therefore, even though we have intelligence, our thoughts and karmas are not appropriate. There is knowledge, but there is narrowness in knowledge, which causes narrowness in karmas and doesn't allow for spontaneity. One who has para buddhi or higher intelligence will not be narrow in knowledge or action. They adopt an expansive outlook and use the intellect in the proper way. They do not get attached to sense objects, but know their nature. Whereas one who exists at the level of apara buddhi is attracted to sense objects and does not know their nature.

Buddhi is a word representing intellect, but intellect is also indicated by the words mudha and viveka. *Mudha* means dumb, dull, inert. One can be intellectual and dumb at the same time when there is no understanding, awareness or realization. The other is *viveka*, where what you have known becomes a discriminative power. In the first case what you know is unknown to you, for you do not have its experience or realization and therefore you are qualified as dumb. This dumbness or dullness is also an expression of the intellect. The other, viveka, the discriminative ability, is also an expression of the intellect.

The higher expression of the intellect is seen when one begins to modify the behaviour of the mind to experience and attain harmony and optimism. But if the awareness is self-centred and self-oriented, then wisdom will only remain an inert knowledge which you will never be able to apply in life. If you look at your own life, you do know what is right and what is wrong, but how many times have you gone on the wrong path knowing fully well that it is not the correct path? Where was the judgement at that time, where was the discrimination, where was the understanding? At that time 'me and my need' overpowered every understanding and knowledge.

The third component of the mind is chitta, which means experience of the internal consciousness. You are able to experience this internal consciousness through memory, *smriti*. You can relive something that happened twenty years ago. Where did that experience come from? From the chitta, which is our storehouse. You put away everything in a storehouse, placing newer things on top of old things, and lock it up. You look for something only when you need it. It's the same with chitta. All the experiences and memories from the time we were born till now are stored in the chitta, and you can take them out whenever you like. You can bring the memory of your wedding day or the birth of your child to the conscious level of the mind and relive the experience of that moment.

Our joys and sorrows are all pasted on this memory board. The wise say that all the impressions and karmas of the past lives are also contained in the chitta. Sometimes when you are sitting in meditation and experiencing immense peace, suddenly a feeling or thought will appear which you were not even aware of. Suddenly you will remember a long-forgotten childhood memory. One of our sannyasins was cured of his asthma when in meditation he suddenly remembered an incident from when he was five years old and his nanny force-fed him. When such events happen, people say it's a miracle, it is guru's grace, he was cured without medicine, but if you try to understand this mystery, you will realize that he was able to cross layer after layer of the mind and dive deep into his chitta so that the suppressed memories came up, and once that impression was taken out of the mind the inner imbalance went away. Memories exist at the conscious, subconscious and unconscious levels. If memories appear in the unconscious they manifest as karmas and if they appear in the conscious, they manifest as knowledge.

The fourth element of the mind is ahamkara. The strongest experience of human life is one's ahamkara, ego. A rock is not as hard as the ego. If a hammer falls on a rock, the rock will shatter, but not so with the ego. And this ego expresses itself in many ways. The first is: "I am important." The feeling in the mind: "I am important." When this feeling exists in the mind, the ego will surface. If you are handed a broom to clean, you will think, "I am being given a broom!" You may not say it aloud, but the thought will appear due to the ego. This thought does not appear due to the manas, buddhi or chitta. For if you take the shelter of buddhi you can accept the broom. You will know that it is meant for a practical purpose and you will not revolt against it. But when the ego holds the broom and not buddhi, then a negative tendency emerges.

Everyone is in the grasp of their ego. One person comes here, you don't look at them – their ego is hurt. Another person comes, they are not offered an asana to sit on, their ego is hurt. The ego does not want to lose its identity ever. Even if one becomes wise, the ego remains. Vishwamitra was a renowned sage, but his ego did not finish. Why? Due to a competitive nature. He continuously compared himself with Rishi Vasishtha – "What qualities does he have that I don't?

Then why do people call him Brahmarshi and call me Rajarshi?" This comparative outlook is the basis of the ego – "He got it, I didn't." There is always a comparison of what another person received and I didn't, and that manifests the ego. And that's where we lose out. Vishwamitra was the drashta of the Gayatri mantra; he had had darshan, but his ego did not finish. Even when a devotee has darshan of God, his ego is not finished. He says, "God, please end the lack in my life." Why? For the fulfilment of ego. The main cause of all comparative and selfish karmas is the ego.

Manas, buddhi, chitta and ahamkara are attached to karmas. The change in the karmas is due to the gunas manifesting in the mind. They are analyzed by the lower mind. They are held within the mind as desire and memory, and the effort to fulfil them is through the ego. These four components of the mind are in two parts: the lower experience and the higher experience. The lower qualities in the lower experience of manas, buddhi, chitta and ahamkara bind one to the world. And the higher qualities of manas, buddhi, chitta and ahamkara liberate one from the world. These are two states of the mind.

All beings are stuck at the lower level, where all propensities are directed towards oneself. At the apara level, self-satisfaction and selfishness are the main feelings. The 'I' element predominates. The thoughts are for pleasure, the efforts are for pleasure, the intellect is used for pleasure, the chitta recalls pleasurable memories and wishes they could be repeated, and ahamkara runs after status, recognition, name and fame. We all live at the level of the lower mind, intelligence, memories and ego. However, the sages say that it is possible to have a higher experience in life, in which you can free yourself from the state of self-orientedness and connect yourself with the transcendental nature and with the sensorial world in an appropriate manner which brings about spiritual, inner evolution. The basis of the sadhanas is to take one away from the lower mind and become established in the higher mind.

At the lower level of the mudha state, the dull and inert state of the mind, intellect, memory and ego, one has to manage the karma of buddhi, chitta, manas and ahamkara. It is this management of the karma created in manas, in buddhi or intellect, in chitta or memories and impressions, and ahamkara or the ego, which is known as karma yoga.

Karma yoga: mind management

Karma yoga is not only physical activity. But all the happenings in the subtle realms through which we are alive are also karma. The gunas, instincts, nature and impressions are subtle, and it is only when they interact with buddhi, chitta and ahamkara that any action begins in life. Until the gunas come into play, the instincts can go on intermingling with each other, no external change will take place. It is all happening inside, there is no outer manifestation. The awareness goes to something only when it manifests. One does not know what is happening to a seed sown in earth; it is only when the sprout emerges that we are able to perceive its development. Many subtle internal activities take place for the sprout to emerge: the hardness of the seed is broken, its potential to become a tree is harnessed and assimilated and then the sprout is able to manifest. No one is aware of the happenings in the subtle realm of the mind; it is perceived when it manifests as a vikara. Here the dealing with mind begins.

We say, "The mind is restless; we need a way to calm it." We try to meditate, as we have learnt that if you meditate, the mind will be calmed. But, when you meditate you only see the *vikara*, the condition of change, you are not able to see its cause. So, you go on struggling with the vikara. Vikara is like the weed in a garden. If you merely snap it from the top but don't unearth its seed from the very depths of the ground, it will continue to appear again and again. Sometimes the roots of a weed can be as deep as three feet and one has to work hard to dig it out. The vikara is like the weed; if you remove it from the top it becomes very small and doesn't catch the eye and you feel that you have been freed of it, but after some time the same vikara-weed, re-emerges.

Sri Swamiji says that if you want peace in the house, the relationship between husband and wife must be congenial. In fights, there are sleepless nights in the house until the matters are resolved fully. Apply the same principle to your mind. Let your relationship with your mind be congenial. Until and unless you come to an agreement with your mind there will be conflict. You spend only sixty or so years with your spouse, but spend your whole life with your mind! If you fight with that which is forever your companion, how will you be at peace?

The peace of your mind is not disturbed by others; it is disturbed by your own mind. You associate the experience of conflict with others, but that is only what appears, the cause of conflict is in fact your own mind. If your mind is not at peace you will spend sleepless nights and if your mind is at peace you will get a good sleep. You blame others; rather blame your own mind. You are not able to understand

58

what you really want. Your lack of understanding is the cause of your suffering, conflict, dislike and hatred. All the negative manifestations arise due to internal conflict.

Why is one jealous of another person? Why is one angry at somebody? Why does one hate somebody? The fault does not lie with the other person; the fault lies in our own mind. So, handle your mind carefully. Come to an agreement with your mind. The day you come to terms with your mind you will not spot any conflict or lack of peace anywhere in the world – neither in your own life nor in the life of your friends, your family, within society or in the world. Rein in your mind properly, don't leave it free. Restrain yourself as much as possible. Practise *sanyam*, restraint, in your thoughts, action and behaviour. If there is restraint the mind is not left free to wander. When the mind is not reined in, it looks for rights. When the mind is controlled, it looks for responsibility.

Therefore, managing and coming to terms with the karmas and behaviour of buddhi, chitta and ahamkara is karma yoga.

Tackling the ego

Manas, buddhi and chitta are the areas where karmas are created, but karmas manifest with the help of ahamkara, ego. Ahamkara gives birth to karmas, as ahamkara is self-identity. In life, it is the ego which plays a crucial role because of the likes and dislikes that it creates within you; the need and ambition, the drive and the motivation that it awakens within you, resulting in either acceptance or rejection of a situation.

Although I have described the full sequence of karma yoga, as an aspirant of spiritual life it is the ego that one has to work with. The primary work has to happen with the ego, as it is from there that karmas manifest in life. I am lecturing here, and if I begin to believe that I am lecturing very well, the ego will naturally be happy. Even at this level of communication the ego is involved. Our responses to life situations are guided by ego. Somebody tells you to do something and immediately a thought comes, "Why me? Why am I targeted? This is not meant to be done by me."

Our perception of ourselves is called self-esteem, which is nothing but an expression of one's ego. People with high self-esteem have bigger egos and those with low self-esteem are also connecting with the negative, lower ego. Confrontation with the ego is what one encounters when involved in karma yoga at the physical level.

Let's say you are a first-timer in the ashram and someone gives you a broom and tells you to sweep the path. You will not like it. You will think, "I have been asked to sweep, I have been asked to clean! They don't know who I am! Many servants are at my beck and call, I have chauffeurs, cars, and these people are telling me to sweep the path?" While this is going on in your mind, another person says to you, "If your sweeping is finished, come and do this folding here." And you think, "What does he think – I am their servant?" Where is that reaction coming from? The ego.

The expression of the ego takes place in the mind, and to fight with the ego is like fighting an elephant. It only ends up hurting you. People say, kill the ego. That is not possible as long as you exist in this body and are drawn to sense enjoyment. Even a sannyasin wants to achieve something due to the ego. It is the ego that ties one down to karma. All have tied themselves and want to be free. First free yourself of the ego eccentricities and then you will be free of suffering, troubles and maya.

The ego is like the dog's tail which can never be straightened; the only way out is to cut it off in one sweep. Why spend years trying to straighten it, just cut off the head of ego. Now what is the sword that can quieten the ego? It is humility. Once you adopt humility in your life the ego will become quiet, and you will save yourself from big trouble. You will not be able to save yourself by practising meditation. Through meditation you can become the witness of the ego, you can see its nature and cause, but you cannot modify it. To modify it, it is necessary to adopt humility.

If someone comes and abuses you, don't accept the abuse. Lord Buddha said to the man who abused him, "I am returning your gift back to you." Retreat gracefully and your mind will remain peaceful, you will not be affected. If you get into a fight to prove your might, you will also get hurt. However, you need to know when to advance and when to retreat; you should have that much discriminative power.

In the ashram, do as the ashramites do. Why do you want to change the system, the disciplines or the structures of the ashram to suit your own need? The ashram is not made to suit your needs; the ashram is for everyone. It exposes you to certain things, it makes you confront certain things in life; accept it, realize it, manage it or you may reject it. If you come to the ashram with the attitude that "I will go to my yoga class, then I will sit in my room and meditate till my next class and everything else will be done for me" – these people have no place in this ashram. Here, try to understand your own nature.

Swami Satyananda's training

The ashram started at Munger in a very humble manner. Today you see the ashram and say, "What a nice place it is!" You do not know how we have lived. When we first came to the ashram, we did not have space to even place our things. We would sleep in the open whether it was winter, monsoon, spring or autumn. In the monsoon we would put plastic sheets over our heads to sleep. We did not have money to buy food. Myself and a few other sannyasins would go to the market and pick up vegetable leaves that were thrown on the road, gather them in a gunny bag, bring them to the ashram, remove the rotten parts, clean the green bits, cook it and eat it. If we had salt it was a feast. Can anybody imagine today that we used to live like that? We have lived in struggle. We never had an easy time. And that allowed us to observe our own mental behaviour. The situations were real. From 1963 to 1977 we were living very simply. The lifestyle changed in 1982 when we shifted from the old ashram to Ganga Darshan. These situations and conditions allowed us to watch ourselves. Every day was a realization of the power and the grip of ego.

Every day was a realization of the hold that the lower buddhi, the lower mind, the lower memories, the lower ego had on us. We had to face it, and because we were able to face it, we are sitting here today. Not because we have practised eight hours of meditation. My achievement is not because of practising meditation. My achievement is because I was taught to confront and face the situations arising in the mind. That is the practical training which I have received, not the meditative training. This training is of karma yoga.

Binding and
Liberating Power of Karma

28th December 2010

Over the last three days we have covered the folowing points:

1. *Four foundations of life*: The birth of the four basic qualities or foundations in life, which become the basis for the experience and unfoldment of life, are the instincts, samskaras, swabhava and the senses.

2. *Gunas*: These are the second level or rung of qualities which intermingle with the first principles, the first operating system. The result of that intermingling process is experienced in the mind.

3. *The mind*: The mind and its various components in the form of manas, buddhi, chitta and ahamkara is where we all experience the karmas that we create in the course of our life. The four foundations and gunas are the subtle aspects of karma which a person does not necessarily know or have access to in order to realize them. They are beyond the range of conscious perceptions and the faculty of intellect, buddhi.

4. *Combination and permutation of systems*: How does one know one's own samskaras? Difficult. How does one know which guna is predominant? Difficult. However, there is predominance of one element, one state of mind all the time. We are unaware of this subtle predominance. The emergence of karma which we begin to perceive, experience and act out in life comes about with the combination and permutation of the first two systems, and the experience is

realized in the mind. We realize that this act, thought, behaviour, desire, etc. is a karma. We realize that it is our duty to perform a karma. We realize that some karmas bind us and some uplift us. This realization of karmas takes place through the mind.

4. *The kitchen of mind*: In the kitchen of mind, ego is the cauldron in which the waters of chitta simmer all the time and in which the grains and vegetables of manas are cooked regularly and spiced by buddhi. These four things coming together give birth to karma awareness, life awareness, ambition awareness, desire awareness. Everything that one aspires for or desires manifests at this level, whether it be material, gross, internal, spiritual or transcendental. There are two levels of the mind, *apara* and *para*, material consciousness and higher consciousness, imprisoned mind and free mind, lower mind and higher mind, the mind engrossed in sense objects and the mind experiencing the spirit. For one to manage the karmas, to make better karmas for oneself, to come to a better level of mind, perception and wisdom, the responses of manas, buddhi, chitta and ahamkara have to change.

5. *Mind management*: The karmas of the mind are managed with pratyahara and dharana. Karmas of buddhi are managed with dharana and dhyana. Karmas of *chitta*, the impressions and memories are managed with visualizations, mantras and yantras. And the karmas of ahamkara have to be managed with the cultivation of the appropriate power which is equal to ego in strength and positive in force. Ego is a negative force. So the force has to be positive and of greater strength than ego, and that force or quality is humility. Ego raises the head; in humility you bend your head.

The binding karma of Prakriti

Remember that karma is universal. We are all part of it; we are an expression of the cosmic karma.

The karma of Prakriti is to give us this gross body. The moment we enter into this gross body we are in the realm of

Prakriti. The moment we adopt *nama, rupa* and *guna*: name, form and quality, we are identified with Prakriti. Prakriti limits the expression of the expansive consciousness. Therefore, although consciousness is all-pervasive and expansive, our understanding and perception of consciousness is limited to our expressions and experiences, limited by our gunas and limited by our nature, impressions, the basic instincts and the senses. This mind with all the four components of reasoning, intelligence, memories and ego is experienced at two levels: the lower mind and the higher mind, the involved mind and the discriminative mind.

We all function at this lower, involved level in life and rarely are we able to raise ourselves up to the higher, discriminative level. Once there was a priest living in a village who would go to different homes to counsel people in times of crises. One day he counselled a bereaved family and gave a beautiful explanation of death so that everyone's spirit was uplifted. On returning home he saw his wife crying because their goat had died. The priest became sad and also started to cry. One of the passers-by who had heard his eloquent speech in the morning stopped and asked what had happened. The priest told him. The passer-by said, "Only a few hours ago you were giving a beautiful sermon about the impermanency of body and eternity of soul!" The priest replied, "That sermon was for the other family, not for me."

The story indicates that even if there is wisdom, when it comes to oneself we come back to the lower state of the mind. Even if there is knowledge, even if there is experience of the higher state, when it comes to our own perceptions and experiences we fall back into the folds of the lower mind. Often, many of the unnecessary things that we are interested in are only for our own satisfaction. We know very well that what we are doing is not correct, but to facilitate certain things for ourselves we willingly push ourselves in, breaching systems and disciplines, ethics and morality. That happens because of the lower mind, the lower buddhi, the lower chitta and the lower ahamkara.

Transcend the lower mind
Karmas are generated in the mind, and one has to work one's way through the expressions and behaviour of the lower mind with awareness and understanding in order to access the higher self. How to have access to the higher self?

Detach and attach: Transcend the limitations of the lower mind, establish yourself in the higher mind so that the expression of manas is higher; not self-oriented, but selfless. The expression of buddhi is not to gratify its own self, but also to make oneself act in a constructive, positive way with the environment and the world. In chitta, the memories which bind us to this life in the form of associations, attachments and identities have to be transcended. Cultivate detachment to move into the higher realms of chitta. When there is attachment we are in the lower realms of chitta. In attachment is *asakti*, identification, with every sensorial pleasure, sense object and oneself. That is the lower expression of chitta. Upon developing the *anasakta bhava*, detachment, subject and object continue to be there but without influence any more. For this to happen, the inner environment has to be balanced.

In the summer you can sit out in the sun only for five minutes but in the winter you can sit out in the sun for a long time comfortably. The sun is the same, but according to the season and environment, at one time you can't be out in the sun for long and at another time you can. The season indicates the mood of nature just as we have moods in our mind. Winter, summer, spring or autumn are different moods of Prakriti. In each season you see a change in the world and a corresponding change in yourself.

Just as the seasons indicate the moods of Prakriti, the different states of perception represent our own moods. Sometimes you blow hot, sometimes you blow cold. All these behaviours are guided by the mood. For a happy person or optimistic person there is happiness all around, and for a frustrated person there is sorrow all around. It's a mood, it's an understanding, it's a perception. By developing detachment from those subjects and objects which cause conflict in life, which bind one to a sense object, to an idea of pleasure, one comes to the upper levels of chitta where our *smriti* is transcendental. When the memories are material, you identify with the material and when the memories are transcendental you identify with that which is non-material and transcendental.

One has to become aware of all the experiences in the apara, the lower state of mind, and then reach higher, to the para state; to rise above the selfish tendency and assume a selfless tendency, to diminish the 'I' tendency and connect with a higher element. What is the higher element beyond buddhi, chitta and ahamkara? It is the *atman*, the spirit. The selfless tendency relates to the spirit.

Re-direct the vrittis: The yoga philosophy says, *Yogashchitta vritti nirodhah* – "Yoga restricts the chitta vrittis". The word that has been used is *nirodha*, restriction, not *avarodha*, cessation, or *virodha*, opposition. Nirodha means changing the direction. The chitta vrittis have been explained as *pramana*, sources of right knowledge, *viparyaya*, misconception, *vikalpa*, unfounded belief, *nidra*, state of sleep, and *smriti*, memory. Smriti is a part of chitta and it is also a vritti. Nidra is an instinct and also a behaviour. When these mental vrittis are redirected inwards towards spirit, a new vritti takes shape, which is called Brahmi vritti.

This is a higher state of mind in which one becomes the *drashta*, witness, of life and at the same time, connects with a higher purpose, *paramartha*. Even while one acts and behaves normally, one is always aware and thinking of a higher purpose. The mind, which was until now connecting with sense objects, now connects with a higher purpose. One crosses the boundaries of material life and becomes established in a higher consciousness in which one experiences the expansiveness of life and spirit, one experiences the expansiveness of the *param tattwa*, supreme element, all the time.

The sages came to the conclusion that all beings have to go through both levels, para as well as apara. Therefore, they advised that for one half of your life, follow the worldly goals, *artha*, material fulfilment, and *kama*, emotional fulfilment; and for the other half of your life perfect the higher expression, *dharma*, righteousness and *moksha*, liberation. The first two are for self-satisfaction and the second two are for a higher expression.

Manage the desires: The root cause of pain and suffering is not because we have desires, every living being has desire, but because we are aware of our desires and they are a strong force. To get to the mind one has to manage the desires. It is not necessary to get rid of them completely, but just as one prunes a tree continuously to maintain it at a certain height, one has to manage the desires in a way that one can perform all the necessary tasks appropriately and also fulfil personal needs.

Everyone has desires, even sannyasins do. The only difference is a sannyasin tries to become a witness of the

desire while a householder is immersed in the desire. It is a
change of mentality, feeling and outlook. So, prune out the
desires that are not beneficial for life and maintain those
that are beneficial. This is how one's mind has to be
redirected from selfishness to selflessness.

Pratyahara and dharana: To organize the karmas of the
mind, thoughts, feelings, the other manifestations of the
mind, it is necessary to practise pratyahara and dharana.

Pratyahara means to prune all that you feed to the mind – all thoughts, all ambitions, all desires, all association with success and failure.

When you get a tiffin full of food, you take out what you need on a plate, repack what is extra and send it back. Applying the same principle to pratyahara, we analyze our thoughts, feelings, emotions, and we sieve out the beneficial from the harmful. This is one meaning of pratyahara, the other is quietening the extrovert tendency of the mind and internalizing the awareness.

Thus, pratyahara means becoming aware of the karmas and holding and acting on that which is useful, and discarding that which is not useful or harmful. Keep throwing out the rubbish of life. The four components of the mind are cleansed with pratyahara and then they become one-pointed in dharana. The state of dharana is where the dissipated energies of the mind are gathered together and focused on one point, one feeling, one thought, one awareness. No restlessness is experienced; instead, there is stillness. To organize the karmas of the mind, to give the right direction to the intellect, the practices of pratyhara and dharana are necessary. As far as dhyana is concerned, it is a state of internal experience where the body consciousness, 'I' consciousness, is absent. With the help of dharana, we can reach the state of dhyana and connect the behaviour of the intellect, which is right now connected with material life, with the higher self.

Chitta shuddhi: For organizing the manas, use pratyahara and dharana; for organizing the buddhi, use dharana and dhyana. For chitta, use chitta shuddhi. Just as information is stored in the computer in an electronic form, life stores information in chitta in the form of memories. These memories pertain not only to this lifetime, but to many lifetimes. However, Nature has locked up this information; otherwise, there will be chaos. Those who have been able to raise themselves from the apara state to the para state can acquire the knowledge of the past, just as Buddha did. For the average person, however, only the active folder is open and we perceive life through it.

The memories in this active folder are coloured by the gunas. When they emerge, they are coloured by the mentality of all our past lives, which do drag us down unwittingly. Therefore, *chitta shuddhi*, or purification of chitta, is necessary for the negative elements from the manifesting memory and experience to be recognized and transformed. Thus one would be able to bring the memories, experiences, impressions and knowledge which are helpful for positive growth to the forefront of awareness.

Tools of mantra, yantra and bhakti: The method to access the chitta is through mantra, yantra and bhakti. Bhakti cleans away the gross emotions and brings spirituality in emotions. Mantras are like a broom for the chitta, yantras bring out the hidden stuff. Just as with a torch one can see the way on a dark road, yantra helps to see the real form of chitta. When we concentrate on a yantra which is appropriate for our sadhana, it realigns the mind, leading to purification of chitta. The first sign of chitta shuddhi is calming and energizing of the mind. This is what mantra achieves. Then one can concentrate on a yantra to enter the deeper regions of chitta. Then, with bhakti, balance and organize the various manifestations of the chitta and make it turn towards God. We connect the chitta to the higher consciousness, we take it from the apara state to the para state and establish it there.

We can practise bhakti towards God, guru or society; whatever method by which everyone is benefited is called bhakti. What is the attainment of bhakti? The *Bhagavad Gita* (12:13) says:

Adveshtaa sarvabhootaanaam maitrah karuna eva cha;
Nirmamo nirahankaarah samaduhkhasukhah kshamee.

He who hates no creature, who is friendly and compassionate to all, who is free from attachment and egoism, balanced in pleasure and pain, and forgiving.

71

Ringing bells, spending time in a temple or contemplating God is only an aspect of bhakti. *Bhakti* is a pure state of mind in which the sense of duality is surpassed; you see yourself in every element, every living being; there is no attachment towards anything, I am free from all, I am friend to all; the compassion in me is flowing towards the whole world, not only towards those dear to me. Do not think of bhakti as worship of God; it is a method to change your life. It is a way, to rise above the sense of duality which keeps assaulting us and to understanding the uniformity of the world. These are the bases of chitta shuddhi.

Evoke the strength of humility: The ego can be quietened with humility. Don't think of humility as a weakness; it is a very powerful force. Only a force that is stronger than the ego that can quieten it. Humility is a power that can free one of the results of the karmas committed due to the ego.

Karma yoga is the way to re-organize manas, buddhi, chitta and ahamkara. Upon balancing of these four, the gunas also acquire balance and the instincts, impressions, nature and sense attachments calm down.

The karmas that are associated with the world, with sense-objects, with God or a higher purpose are being produced in the mind. *Yoga* means to join, to come close and become one. Karma yoga is when a state of equilibrium and balanced expression comes about in the karmas. As long as there is disturbance and dissipation in the karmas, it is karma. Until now all have been performing karma – following the dictates of manas, buddhi, chitta and ahamkara. Ahamkara says, "He is humiliating you. Give him two slaps," and we go and do that. Buddhi says, "That's a beautiful car. If you acquire it, you will be known all over the town," and we go and buy it. The karmas that you perform through your attachments with the world are karmas of the apara state. When you want to be free of karmas and achieve a state of equanimity, when you want integration between material and spiritual levels, then you have to come to the para state. That is the principle of karma yoga.

Cultivate faith and commitment

It is these inner attitudes that one has to confront. By being in situations where you are not in control, you confront your own nature. Where you are in control, there is no need to confront your nature, you can weave your way as required. But, when you are not in control of the situation and have to listen to someone else, your boss or master, at one point there will be rejection to his mandate. To not have that rejection, one has to cultivate faith and commitment.

You have heard the story of Milarepa, the saint of Tibet, and his guru, Marpa. Marpa did not allow him to come for any spiritual lessons, but asked him to work hard. He asked him to make a stone hut on top of a mountain and once it was ready he asked him to bring it down, stone by stone, and build another one at another location. Again and again he asked him to repeat this process. Then one day, Marpa gave Milapepa a shove off the mountainside for being too lazy and Milarepa fell down the precipice. As he was falling, all he could think was, "I have not completed the mandate given to me by my guru." And, before his body hit the rocks below, an invisible hand appeared, stopped his fall, lifted him up and placed him standing before his guru. Marpa then said, "Milarepa, today you have become greater than me."

Would you, in the position of Milarepa, have laboured in that manner to fulfil the command of a guru? No. Nobody can do that. The guru saw the potential in Milarepa. He saw that it is through exhaustion of karma and not meditation that he could make him greater than himself. Swami Sivananda said the same thing to Swami Satyananda, "Work hard, just involve yourself in karma yoga and the light within you will shine." It was the guru who recognized the quality in a disciple and instigated that quality to germinate.

The search for liberation

The *prarabdha karma*, the destined karma with which we come into this life gives a direction, a goal, a purpose to life, an independent direction to develop. Many times the natural direction of life is diverted by the impositions of education, society and family. One moves in a diverted direction in life and accumulates yet another set of karmas.

We have come into this world to be free and follow our own destined path in life. The spirit seeks freedom. The spirit will avoid situations where it is bound. The desire for liberation is seen as mukti or moksha. If there was no demand by the spirit to liberate itself from gross karmic bondage, the concept of moksha and mukti would never arise. If there was no ill health, the medical science would never have come about. Medical science came about because we want to be freed from the effects of ill health. The spiritual sciences developed because we want to be free from the gross materialistic associations and bondages of society, family and the world.

We play many roles in life. We played a certain role when we were children, we became different when we grew up and when we matured. The process of thinking changed, the attractions changed, the ideas changed, the beliefs changed. In each situation, in each condition we have behaved differently. The difference in behaviour is maturity, gaining a better understanding than what one had before. Maturity is developing a better understanding while lack of understanding is immaturity.

Five types of karma

Look at the varieties of karma – how many types of karmas are seen when they become manifest?

Selfish and selfless karma: The ego and mental karmas manifest as selfish karmas. They are called sakama karma, which are performed to satisfy our own needs and ambitions. Another category of karma is nishkama or selfless karma, which is performed to help others. *Sakama* means with desire and *nishkama* means no desire. Nishkama karma is not meant for oneself. Whatever I do for myself will always be sakama. I desire food, I desire clothes, I desire comfort; as long as the idea is 'I desire', it is always towards oneself. That is

74

called self-oriented, sakama. The other is nishkama, without desire. 'Without desire' does not mean absence of desire in the mind; rather, those desires are not pointing towards oneself. The desire is there, but it is not directed towards oneself for personal good, but for greater good.

Social karma: The second type of karma is social karma. There is a word in Hindi, *paropkara*, for the benefit of others. An action which has a greater reach, not on a one-to-one basis, but encompasses the society at large, that is social karma. Living the social paropkara karmas are necessary to overcome the vritti of self-oriented awareness, which is identified with desire.

If you look at the social traditions and lives of the luminaries of spiritual traditions, you will discover that at some point in their life they all involved themselves in paropkara, whether it be St. Francis of Assisi, Swami Sivananda or Swami Satyananda.

The power of compassion which propels one to serve is called paropkara. It is *samajik karma*, actions related to the welfare of society. Society does not only comprise of human beings. Many spiritual luminaries have offered their service to insects, birds and animals and protected them; for the feeling of compassion that emanates from within is for all life forms in creation.

Many luminaries have helped life forms which are mute and dumb. They cannot express the suffering which they are feeling, but are suffering nevertheless. Many saints have identified with that suffering, with nurturing the spirit in that particular life form. There are people who identify with the human groups, there are those who identify with the animal groups, there are people who identify with birds and insects.

These karmas are further strengthened by the force of faith, *shraddha*. You can go into real paropkara when there is faith. Without faith you just end up creating a social club for your own gains and ends. It is only when faith becomes part of the act, that the action becomes paropkara. Buddha gave this message to his disciples: *Bahujan hitaya, bahujan sukhaya* – "For the welfare of many and for the pleasure of many," O sadhu, O sannyasi, O bhikku, keep on working, keep on striving, keep on walking. Paropkara is where you express the divine qualities that are inherent in you, bring them to life and connect yourself with everyone. Swami Sivananda said that the ultimate aim of spiritual life is to serve, love and give.

Destined karma: The third kind of karma is the destined karma, *prarabdha karma*. What is destined? Laws of nature and the effect of those laws on human existence – that is prarabdha karma. What is the prarabdha karma of the body? What is the destined karma of the body? Birth, sickness, decay and death. No one can change this karma. One cannot stop the body from decaying and ageing no matter how many lotions one puts on the face and body, or how many hours are spent at the gym or on a diet. Despite every effort, the body is going to deteriorate day by day. That is the karma of the body and nothing will change this prarabdha karma. Same thing with the mind. No matter what you do to please it, the mind which is under the law of Prakriti will continue to develop in its own way. One does not have any control on prarabdha karmas, on the destined karmas. These destined karmas are related to birth, sickness, decay and death only.

Sanchita karma: The fourth type of karma is sanchita karma. It refers to those karmas, experiences or involvements in life which have been registered by one's consciousness, but have not been able to influence one's life as yet. They are somewhere there, just like a fixed deposit which has not matured, they are the actions done in previous lives. Whatever you did in your previous life is embedded in your subconscious mind. It remains there and is called sanchita karma or accumulated action.

It is impossible to exhaust prarabdha karma; destiny is unalterable, but the other karmas can be changed. If there are certain samskaras in your subconscious mind and you do not want them to fructify, you can immediately remove them if you know the method. You can interfere with your subconscious stuff, you can also interfere with the present karmas in the conscious mind, but you cannot interfere with the prarabdha karmas that have to come to you in the form of suffering and enjoyment. If you interfere, they will come back with double force.

Daiva karma: The fifth type of karma is daiva karma, to cultivate the awareness of the transcendental nature, divinity or purity in life. Your spiritual sadhana is daiva karma. Meditation is a daiva karma, a sadhana to experience the transcendental quality of life. The desire to attain harmony and peace, and the right, appropriate effort that you make towards this aim is daiva karma. To create a state of tranquillity, peace, harmony and luminosity is daiva karma.

Therefore, to live life according to the laws of nature is prarabdha karma. To work for the welfare of others by cultivating positive strengths such as compassion, sympathy and understanding is paropkara karma, social karma. To help somebody come out of the misery that they may be experiencing in their life at that particular moment is nishkama karma. And to help oneself attain a goal for oneself is sakama karma.

Interaction with the five karmas

Our role, our involvement in karma is only between sakama, self-oriented, nishkama, selfless, and paropkara, welfare. These are the three areas of human interaction – me, the

77

other person and the group. As for prarabdha karma, the body just lives it out, the hair turn grey and wrinkles appear.

Cosmic karma or daiva karma is only performed by one who has surrendered to the higher course. Then God takes over and uses you as the instrument to bring forth the melody which God wants to play. As the prayer by St.Francis says – *Make me an instrument of Thy peace*. It will only happen when total surrender has taken place, not before. Not as long as you are working with your ego. We work with our ego at all levels of karma – the selfish, selfless and welfare-oriented. There is no ego in prarabdha because you don't know what. it is, how to manage or control it. And there is no ego in daiva karma because you are not the doer, God or guru is the instructor.

Despite the picture created over these four days, the area of focus is limited to ego, selfish karma, selfless karma and welfare karma. I have given you the full map of karma, but now I am telling you to concentrate and focus on the perimeter of ahamkara, sakama, nishkama and paropkara. Manage these four components effectively, then you become a karma yogi. When we are able to manage them, we develop immunity to the responses of the world. To develop immunity is very difficult, for everyone is a very sensitive creation.

Once a person came to me and said, "Swamiji, I am suffering from hypertension." I asked, "Do you remember the cause of your hypertension? How did it first start?" He said, "Yes, I remember. I retired about six months ago and one day I was sitting at home having my tea, reading the newspaper and watching the morning news. And my daughter-in-law, who was in a foul mood that day, was vacuuming the room. And I heard her mutter under her breath, 'My father-in-law sits like a dog on the sofa.' I did not say anything to her, but I still carry the pain and hurt of that statement in my heart and I know it to be the cause of my hypertension. What practices can I do?" I asked, "When she said you sit like a dog, what kind of image came to your mind about the dog?" He said, "Oh, the street dog." So I told him, "Your hypertension is not because of what your daughter-in-law said to you, but because you created an image of the dog for yourself within your mind and you are identifying with that image." He asked, "Swamiji, what can I do to overcome this problem?" I said, "Continue to think that you are a dog, but instead of a street dog, be the dog of a memsahib who lives in an air-conditioned house, who is served food on time, who travels in an air-conditioned car with dignity, who has no lack in life. Cultivate this image in your mind about yourself, and clear the impression of the sickly-looking dog." The person returned after a month. I had forgotten about the incident, and he said, "Swamiji, my hypertension is gone. I followed the advice you gave. I became the dog of a memsahib and now I don't have high blood pressure."

Develop immunity and flow with karma
The story is an example of an ego reaction to a person, to a statement. Anything that affects the ego in a negative way creates a mark which is binding, and anything that affects the ego in a constructive, positive way is a karma that frees the ego from bondage. People should involve themselves in *satkarma*, positive karma. The spiritual traditions of India do not advocate meditation, they advocate satkarma. Meditation is only a means to develop the concept, the understanding, the awareness and the qualities to perform karma in the appropriate manner.

The person in the story suffered because of a statement of his daughter-in-law. He was not immune to her statement and was hurt by that. If somebody tells me, "You are a donkey," I will say, "Only a donkey can recognize another donkey!" I won't believe the statement or be dejected and depressed because somebody abused me. I will say, "All right, he sees me as a donkey, I know that I am not a donkey, so why should I be affected?" He is saying something in a reaction and I am understanding that with my wisdom.

Problems arise when you confront a reaction and react to reaction. When you accept and understand a karma, there is harmony, but when you react against karma, problems will arise.

Through the fine-tuning of our nature, through the practices of yoga and fine-tuning of our karmas by cultivating a balanced attitude and awareness, we learn how to flow in life with ease and grace, understanding and wisdom. That learning is known as karma yoga. It is harmony of karmas which are performed unconsciously, subconsciously and consciously through the body, mind and ego.

One learns from all the different exposures one receives. When you are able to confront the exposures and crises that you come across in life in a positive way, it becomes a learning process. The aim is to follow the human dharma, not contradict it. When you follow the human dharma, when you flow with ease and grace in life, when you cultivate understanding and awareness, then you are free. If you don't follow your dharma and don't apply your *jnana*, wisdom, then karma will bind you.

Karma fructifies only when it is attached to dharma. Therefore, to harmonize karmas, know the human dharma first. Human dharma is the inherent responsibility. When karma and dharma unite, the karma changes, it becomes *kartavya*, duty. To perform a karma as duty, it is necessary to attach it with dharma. The word 'dharma' is not being used here in the sense of religion; *dharma* is our natural responsibility. To come to terms with karma, make duty the primary component and not the karma. Attach yourself with responsibility as in that there is a beautiful union of karma and dharma. With this union, everything flows naturally, the plans get made, the actions are performed, the results come about and life progresses.

When you look after your home and family, educate your children, you do it as your duty, the feeling of kinship makes you constantly aware of what's going on. If something goes wrong, you are immediately involved and see that involvement as your responsibility. If two members of the family are fighting, you go and tell them, "Don't fight," and see it as your responsibility to do so, you don't see it as karma. Therefore, any karma that brings out the dharma through which harmony and a positive environment are created is duty. This duty is to be connected with all five types of karma.

If you are able to see all that you do in life not as karma but as kartavya, then you are a karma yogi. Thus, to become a karma yogi is as simple as perfecting karma. How? Become like the tree which will give its fruits irrespective of who climbs up to pluck them, who throws a stone to bring them down or who cuts the tree to pick the fruits. In every condition, the duty of the tree is to give fruits. Nature always follows duty and a human being follows karma. Nature looks upon everyone equally, but a human being holds himself as primary on the basis of karmas. When duty is followed everyone receives equal importance. The simple way to become a karma yogi is to connect the karmas with dharma. If you want to become a karma yogi through sadhana, if you want to progress by calming the dissipations of your life, then come to terms with the four aspects of the mind, in which the biggest adjustment has to be made with ego.

The last block is the ego. The ego causes the maximum pain, because it makes you aware of yourselves, it makes you aware of your position, your name and fame. It takes us to the peak level of the experience of our self. And it is this ego that binds a person to the karmas and makes them turn away from dharma. That is why we are not able to see a karma as responsibility, but think of it as a burden. And the ego is fed with desires.

To manage the ego, it is necessary to come to terms with oneself. For as long as there is ego, you will continue to react to your environment. In reaction, only the negative conditions of the mind will be expressed. There will be continuous action and reaction in life and conflicts with others. You will react to what others say or do and then go and try to trouble them in turn. Until the ego is tackled, you cannot come to an agreement; when there is no ego, an agreement is reached and karma turns into karma yoga.

Go on following the human dharma, don't allow the ego to raise its head, get to know the circumstances, thought processes and needs of others, and even as you work for your own welfare, strive to work for others' growth also. These are the signs of a karma yogi and this is an internal process through which one can make the character pure and calm.

So, when we add the word 'yoga' to 'karma', it means acquiring the ability to observe, understand and flow with ease and grace through life by cultivating immunity to the sensitive nature of the mind and sensitive expressions of the ego, the aggressive behaviour of the ego. We try to make our actions positive, liberating, constructive and perfect. This is the whole process of karma yoga.